SpongeBob SquarePants
and Philosophy

Popular Culture and Philosophy®
Series Editor: George A. Reisch

For full details of all Popular Culture and Philosophy® books, visit www.opencourtbooks.com.

Popular Culture and Philosophy®

SpongeBob SquarePants and Philosophy

Soaking Up Secrets Under the Sea!

Edited by
JOSEPH J. FOY

OPEN COURT
Chicago and LaSalle, Illinois

Volume 60 in the series, Popular Culture and Philosophy®,
edited by George A. Reisch

This book has not been prepared, endorsed, or
authorized by the creators, producers, or distributors of
SpongeBob SquarePants.

**To order books from Open Court, call toll-free 1-800-815-2280, or visit our
website at www.opencourtbooks.com.**

Open Court Publishing Company is a division of Carus Publishing Company.

Copyright © 2011 by Carus Publishing Company

First printing 2011

Printed and bound in the United States of America.

Library of Congress Cataloging-in-Publication Data

SpongeBob SquarePants and philosophy : soaking up secrets under the sea!
/ edited by Joseph J. Foy.
    p. cm.— (Popular culture and philosophy ; v. 60)
  Includes bibliographical references and index.
  ISBN 978-0-8126-9730-8 (trade paper : alk. paper)
  1. SpongeBob SquarePants (Television program). I. Foy, Joseph J.
PN1992.77.S68S68 2011
791.45'72—dc23

                                                      2011017173

To Connor Joseph,

May you always greet the world with a smile,
a song, and the feeling that you are ready.

—Love, Daddy

*You must learn to be
a sponge, if you want to
be loved by hearts that
overflow.*

—Friedrich Nietzsche,
Thus Spoke Zarathustra

SPONGEBOB: Quick, Patrick, without thinking! If you could have anything right now, what would it be?

PATRICK: Um . . . More time for thinking.

—"Chocolate with Nuts," 2002

Contents

PART II

Welcome to Bikini Bottom   85

PART III

You're Like a Steamed Vegetable, Only Smarter   153

Acknowledgments

I want to begin by thanking the contributors to this volume. Your enthusiasm for the project made working on this book a true delight, and I appreciate your efforts and many superb insights into this beloved show. I would also like to express my thanks and gratitude to George Reisch and the good people at Open Court for embracing this volume, as well as for their patience and guidance along the way. Thank you to my friends at the University of Wisconsin-Waukesha and across the University of Wisconsin System. I want to express my gratitude in particular to Dean A. Kowalski, without whom I would likely never have had such wonderful opportunities. Thanks to my parents, Sue and Jim, brother Shawn, and sisters Leah and Keri for always allowing me to be who I am (and loving me all the same). I hope you can share this book with my special nieces and nephew so that they know their Uncle Joe is thinking of them. Finally, no words could even begin to express my sincere appreciation for my wife Kristi and son Connor whose patience and understanding teach me what is truly important in this world.

Who Teaches Philosophy Under the Sea?

In 1999, following the *Nickelodeon Kids' Choice Awards*, the world was greeted by a portrait of a pirate with moving lips asking if we were ready. Ready for what? Little did audiences know that they were about to meet a little yellow sponge who would make history for children's programming and leave a lasting mark on audiences across the globe.

SpongeBob SquarePants, which recently celebrated its eleventh year on the air, is a proven staple of American and international popular culture. One can hardly walk into a shopping center, bookstore, market, or preschool, elementary school (or in some cases, college) classroom without being greeted by happy images of SpongeBob, and a favorite image of mine to show my classes is graffiti from a wall in Mexico with a crudely spray-painted SpongeBob caricature with the words "Bob Esponja Presidente" or "SpongeBob for President."

Although it debuted in relative obscurity, by its second season *SpongeBob SquarePants* saw an enormous growth in viewership and ratings. It has continued in its popularity for the past decade. Most notably, nearly nine million viewers tuned in to view the November 12th, 2007, *Atlantis SquarePantis*, a musical film guest starring the legendary David Bowie. According to sources at Nickelodeon, nearly forty-five million people over the age of eighteen watch *SpongeBob* every month, and President Barack Obama and the first family, actress Scarlett Johansson, actor Johnny

Depp, and basketball icon LeBron James all count themselves among the millions of fans of the show. Likewise, the popularity of the series is matched only by its critical acclaim. At the time of this book's production, *SpongeBob* has taken home over forty major production awards since its debut, including seven Emmy Awards (four straight from 2007 to 2010). Syracuse University Professor Robert Thompson—perhaps the most notable scholar in the field of popular culture studies in the United States today—says it's impossible to overestimate how much *SpongeBob* has penetrated American culture.

A major part of *SpongeBob's* appeal is that it draws an audience of all age groups. As Thompson said in a National Public Radio *Morning Edition* program celebrating ten years of *SpongeBob*:

> You watch when you're a little kid and you like it because it's pretty and it's funny and they do goofy things. You watch it again when you're ten, and suddenly all of the new mysteries of life begin to pop up in here as well. And then you watch it when you're a twenty-one year-old in a frat house and suddenly there's a whole other quality that appeals to you.[1]

But just what are these "other qualities" that people find so appealing? What is it about the antics of SpongeBob SquarePants and his friends in Bikini Bottom that have people from eight to eighty tuning in at such high volume?

The contributors to this book make a strong case that what keeps SpongeBob "reeling in" major audiences on a daily basis is that underneath the lighthearted and whimsical exterior are the seeds of long-standing and important philosophical discussions about identity and the self, our

---

[1] Elizabeth Blair, "SpongeBob: Still Soaking Up Ratings After 10 Years," *NPR*, <www.npr.org/templates/story/story.php?storyId=103170924>.

obligations toward others, benefits and tensions of the individual in community, principles of the marketplace and environmental ethics, and questions of just how exactly Jack Kahuna Laguna can build a fire at the bottom of the ocean. (Okay, so perhaps we don't have an answer for that last one, but maybe if you look into that fire long enough the answer will be revealed.)

Collectively, this book's designed to introduce fans of *SpongeBob SquarePants* to some of the great thinkers and questions in philosophy. And, like the series, the contributors of this volume have attempted to make their chapters ones that can be shared by the young and old alike, hopefully kindling new interest in philosophy and life's big questions. So, to all you Goofy Goobers out there, enjoy the antics of your favorite yellow sponge in square-shaped pants and all of his friends (and enemies, lest we forget about the likes of Plankton and Man Ray).

Perhaps in the laughter and entertainment we can discover a little bit more about ourselves during our time under the sea. With that there's but one question left to ask: Are you ready, kids?

PART I

I'm Ready, I'm Ready, I'm Ready

1
Self-Mastered Sponge

NICOLE R. PRAMIK

No doubt about it, SpongeBob SquarePants is happy. Every morning when his foghorn alarm blasts, SpongeBob springs out of bed with a smile on his face and a song on his lips. Not the normal reaction we might expect from a minimum-wage fry cook who calls a pineapple home. However, as SpongeBob sings in the episode "Truth or Square," "When you're doing something that you really love, and so proud of, then work is like play." Our porous, yellow friend is smiling because he is living a good life.

Like SpongeBob, the Greek philosopher Aristotle (384–322 B.C.E.) also felt that the good life was the life of happiness. However, rather than just a life of pleasure-seeking and wish-fulfillment, Aristotle described happiness as a state of *eudaimonia*, which means flourishing or living well. Such a state is achieved when a person lives a virtuous life defined by a middle path between extremes of excess or deficiency, what he famously referred to as the "golden mean."

Throughout his many adventures under the sea, SpongeBob demonstrates a life of well-being. He may on occasion fall short of virtue, but from his shortcomings he learns that the true road to happiness is becoming a self-mastered sponge. SpongeBob, more than any other character in Bikini Bottom, serves as a representation of Aristotle's philosophy on happiness and the good life. Aristotle may have written that "happiness then is the best, noblest, and most pleasant thing in the world" (*Nichomachean Ethics*, Book I, Section 8) but SpongeBob shows us how to serve it up on a sesame seed bun.

We Could Teach You How to Be Good

Aristotle's views on ethics and happiness are based on his ideas about virtue and vice, both of which are states of existence. Vice is acting on one of two extremes, either an extreme of excess (such as Mr. Krabs's obsession with wealth) or an extreme of deficiency (like Patrick's lack of, shall we say, "intellectual awareness"). Virtue, on the other hand, is the middle path; a position Aristotle calls the "golden mean" or moderation. Aristotle claimed that choosing to act and behave in accordance with this mean leads to virtue, which is the way people should live. Extremes, or vices, are undesirable since they reveal an inability to keep one's self in check. Whether through overkill or complacency, extremes indicate that a person is not in control of her life, while living in accordance with the mean results in virtue.

But virtue is not something you either have or you don't. You have to practice and act on it, much like a muscle must be toned and exercised before it can effectively bear weight. The more you act on virtue, the more likely you are to respond in given situations with virtuous behaviors or attitudes. But the more you act and respond in accordance with vices, the more likely your virtue muscle will become flabby. And no pair of anchor arms will be of much help! Exercising moderation and self-control, Aristotle argues, leads to a virtuous, happy life.

Like SpongeBob, Aristotle seeks happiness as the chief good. He defines it as both what "we choose always for its own sake, and never with a view to anything further" and "something final and self-sufficient" (Book I, Section 7). In other words, happiness is a good in itself. It needs nothing else to give it value, and it's the final goal of any virtuous attitude or behavior. When SpongeBob wakes up each morning and greets the day, he does so with a smile simply because he is living a moral, happy life. His contentment extends into his view of his own mortality, such as when he tells Squidward, "if I were to die in some fiery explosion due to the carelessness of a friend . . . well, that would just be okay" ("Dying for Pie"). SpongeBob isn't being flippant here. He's expressing how fulfilling and flourishing his life is. He doesn't need anything extra to make him happy, and his happiness doesn't need any other reasoning.

Behaving and acting virtuously leads to a good, happy life. Giving into vice leads to a warped view of both the self and life and leads in the opposite direction of happiness. In SpongeBob's case, giving in to vice, which he occasionally does, leads to suffering or sadness. A classic case of this occurs in "The Card" where SpongeBob goes on the fixated hunt for an ultra-rare talking Mermaid Man #54 trading card. His search leads him to squander his money and sob when Patrick recklessly destroys his own card (before informing SpongeBob that he has more). A similar situation arises in "Waiting" when SpongeBob obsesses about waiting for a toy in the mail, only to end up in tears when Patrick (supposedly) breaks it. Thankfully, SpongeBob learns from the unhappiness he endures when he doesn't act virtuously, which sets him back on the path to a good life. When he acts virtuously, he receives the fruits of his labor through happiness.

SpongeBob exemplifies someone who seeks to live within the means of virtue and avoid the vices of extremes.

Like any of us, SpongeBob is not perfect. Most of his lessons (both to himself and the audience) come as the result of not doing the right thing the first time around. It's through these lapses in judgment that SpongeBob realizes how to live a better life and attain happiness. To his credit, he gives it his best effort to live virtuously—even if he does have the occasional backslide. Aristotle noted that a self-mastered life is attained through the practice of virtue. Arguably, one of SpongeBob's most attractive featured is that he does mess up from time to time, just like we do. But while SpongeBob's "virtue muscle" isn't fully toned and bulked up, he's certainly not slacking on exercising it. Like the average "land creature" (that's us!), SpongeBob strives to exude good character and attain happiness in his life.

Licking Doorknobs Is Illegal on Other Planets

What should SpongeBob do to live a virtuous and happy life? Aristotle claims that virtue exists through moderation in four behavioral characteristics: courage, honor, truth, and anger. In SpongeBob's sundry adventures (and misadventures) under the sea, he displays these four qualities on many occasions. When he loses control of himself, he suffers. When he exhibits a dedication to the "golden mean," we can see him living a happy, virtuous life.

The extremes of courage, which in this case is the virtuous mean, are cowardliness (fear of everything) and rashness (no fear at all). Courage doesn't often come automatically for SpongeBob, but he eventually realizes that facing obstacles and exiting his comfort zone are necessary to save the day and restore happiness. Doing the right thing trumps being afraid. One such example in "I Had an Accident" would be when SpongeBob shatters his (ahem) posterior in a sandboarding accident and becomes afraid of permanently breaking his rump and having to live in an "iron butt." Out of fear, SpongeBob isolates himself from the outside world to prevent another accident. He hides inside his pineapple, making friends with a used napkin, a potato chip, and a penny out of a sense of cowardly paranoia. However, when Sandy and Patrick are attacked by a gorilla on his doorstep, SpongeBob feels compelled to leave the security of his home and save them. He acts courageously by facing his fears and achieves happiness in the knowledge that his friends are safe and the world is not so dangerous after all. Living in fear and isolation, SpongeBob learns he can't achieve the quality life he desires. This state of deprivation keeps him from everything and everyone he enjoys and loves being around. However, courage allows him to regain these things and relationships, opening the door (literally, in this case) to a happy life.

But sometimes courage gives way to recklessness. SpongeBob shows this extreme when he takes Larry the Lobster's challenge to embrace a life of danger ("A Life in a Day"). At first, SpongeBob is worried about this type of lifestyle, especially as he witnesses Patrick put his life at blatant risk. In time, SpongeBob gives into the adrenaline-driven pursuits, which lands both him and Patrick in the hospital. True courage doesn't mean "no fear." Instead, courage must be tempered with a concern for safety and common sense. In order to be happy, SpongeBob must seek the "golden mean" between fear and recklessness.

SpongeBob purposefully avoids recklessness in "Pre-Hibernation Week" when Sandy recruits him to join her in a series of extreme sports, from searching for a piece of hay in a needle stack to biking through a toxic industrial park. While Sandy displays the extreme of recklessness, SpongeBob remains convinced that "This squirrel's trying to kill me." Her idea of fun is, to him, quite dangerous. He finally decides to opt out of her excursions of excessiveness by declaring he won't play with her anymore as these "games are tearing me apart!"

To his credit, SpongeBob often displays genuine courage. Some classic cases are when he forced himself to navigate the dark and strange Rock Bottom after missing a bus ride home ("Rock Bottom") and when he resolved to return to the Krusty Krab after an über-picky customer complains about his cooking ("Pickles"). He also tackled a bubble-popping street gang ("WhoBob WhatPants") and braved an alternative Medieval universe to battle a monster jellyfish ("Dunces and Dragons"). On a larger scale, in *SpongeBob SquarePants: the Movie*, SpongeBob decides to not cower in fear at King Neptune's threats to destroy Mr. Krabs for allegedly stealing his crown. Instead, SpongeBob acts courageously and sets out for Shell City. Overall, SpongeBob doesn't behave as if there's nothing to fear and often runs from what scares him only to learn courage later, proving he's not afraid to stand up for himself or others.

The next behavior Aristotle explores is honor, which is defined as the middle position between excessive humility and empty vanity. On the first extreme, excessive humility, a person would feel demeaned. On the second, extreme vanity, a person acts like a braggart. Both are considered vices as they reveal a person possesses either too little or too much value of herself or himself. SpongeBob strives to live in accordance with the "golden mean" of honor as he demonstrates greatness of the soul, shown chiefly in how he views himself. SpongeBob retains a rather high, healthy self-esteem.

There are exceptions, of course. One such case would be "Something Smells" where SpongeBob discovers his bad breath is keeping everyone at bay. Patrick, who has no nose, asserts, "Maybe it's because you're ugly," which sends SpongeBob into a downward spiral where he loathes himself. But, once he realizes the fact of the matter, he reverts to his usual, sunny disposition and regains the virtuous mean by restoring his personal honor.

There are times when SpongeBob behaves dishonorably. He brags that he's "a jerk" when sporting plastic blow-up muscles and showing off ("MuscleBob BuffPants") and allows a few nanoseconds of fame to go to his head ("As Seen on TV"). He even lets Plankton talk him into being rude to others under the guise of self-assertion ("Walking Small") and slights Sandy both by telling jokes that demean her intelligence ("Squirrel Jokes") and when he proclaims himself as "king of karate" ("Karate Island"). In all of these scenarios, SpongeBob displays less than his best when it comes to honor. Thankfully, he doesn't stay that way. He learns his lesson when his vanity causes him to fall on his face. His big-headed antics are momentary and cause him to be deprived of the true happiness he craves. He redeems his honor by deciding to behave rightly in the mean and apologizing so relationships can be restored.

Regarding honor, it's interesting to consider SpongeBob's neighborhood, which represents Aristotle's ideas at work. First, there's Patrick who has a tendency to belittle himself (even jokingly doing so) for his lack of intelligence and personal motivation ("Dumb people are always blissfully unaware of how dumb they really are"). His deficiencies of honor are symbolized by the fact he resides under a rock. Patrick's home signifies he likes being kept down and in the dark. On the other hand, there's persnickety Squidward in his lofty Easter Island head, whose best friend is himself. His vanity is equally represented in his numerous self-portraits and sculptures. Playing on the idea of the stereotypical snobby artist, Squidward looks down his giant nose at everyone else, thus inflating his own self-importance, though he is neither better nor worse off than anyone else. Unlike Patrick and Squidward, his neighbors of extremes, SpongeBob works to display honor by taking pride in his boating school studies, work, and personal appearance, yet seeks to avoid putting himself on a pedestal.

SpongeBob equally feels the need to maintain a sense of truth, which is the mean between never speaking one's mind and *braggadocio*, boastfully speaking too much of one's mind. Truth often comes through SpongeBob's interactions with his friends. While he certainly isn't willing to be so honest he purposely hurts feelings, he tries to tread the high road by admitting when either he or someone else is wrong.

He doesn't always tell the truth right away. For example, he allows Patrick to help him cheat during a boating exam by using a radio in his head ("Boating School"), lies about playing on fishing hooks after Mr. Krabs warns him not to ("Hooky"), and initially tries to cover up smeared paint on Mr. Krabs's first dollar ("Wet Painters"). In these cases, SpongeBob doesn't immediately admit the truth—though his conscience eventually gets the better of him and he confesses, thus putting him back on the virtuous track of honesty.

Guilt drives him to admit he's cheating during the boating exam, especially after Mrs. Puff expresses confidence in him, which SpongeBob knows he hasn't fairly earned. This makes him upset and sad, displacing his ability to live a life of happiness until he can redeem himself. Likewise, his quasi-paternal bond with Mr. Krabs ultimately prevents him from carrying on a falsehood for too long, and this leads him to tell the truth about how he disobeyed by playing with the hooks and accidently getting paint on his boss's most prized possession. In the former episode "Hooky," SpongeBob's disrobing (in order to be free of a hook embedded in his clothes) symbolizes the stripping down of his soul during these times of less than perfect honesty. This ability to feel shame, which Aristotle likens to a virtue, places SpongeBob on the path to virtue and happiness.

When SpongeBob acts honestly, he stands up for truth even when it does not immediately serve him. SpongeBob is honest with his friends when he feels they've crossed the line, but he expresses himself in a way that seeks to impart truth to others as opposed to just being frank to build up his own ego. In "Rule of Dumb," when Patrick's newly-found kingly power corrupts him, SpongeBob tactfully tells him he's "kind of being a jerk" for Patrick's own good. Likewise, he confronts Mr. Krabs, admitting he can't publish nor write the tabloid-esque stories for the newly-created "Krabby Kronicle" just to make a buck ("The Krabby Kronicle"). In this case, SpongeBob initially goes along with the idea to embellish mundane stories when Mr. Krabs assures him that imagination isn't harmful. But when SpongeBob sees that his sensationalized stories are ruining reputations and hurting feelings, he suffers the torment of knowing he is inflicting the damage. This leads him to confront his boss and turn the presses against Krabs. In these cases and others, SpongeBob demonstrates modest candidacy rather than his ego to make sure he tells the truth for good ends. He discovers that being honest makes himself, and in the long-run everyone else, happy.

SpongeBob also shows virtuous judgment when it comes to anger. He neither never gets angry (one extreme) nor does he exhibit unadulterated rage (the other extreme). Instead, he frequently engages in the virtuous mean of good-temper. Good-temper does not mean never getting angry or behaving like a wimp. Aristotle labels those actions vices because there are situations that, out of a sense of justice, deserve getting upset about. But the virtuous person knows how to channel anger into a productive instrument. In SpongeBob's case, his anger is usually directed at some sort of unfortunate incident or injustice, such as getting into an argument with Patrick if he feels he's been wronged. When SpongeBob and Patrick do fight, whether it's over a missing jellyfishing net ("The Pink Purloiner"), Patrick's lack of personal hygiene ("The Battle of Bikini Bottom"), or a commitment to caring for a baby scallop ("Rock-a-Bye Bivalve"), their fights ultimately produce nothing and prevent either of them from attaining happiness.

One great example of how SpongeBob experiences and productively deals with anger is in "New Student Starfish" where he and Patrick attend boating school together. Patrick gets SpongeBob into trouble, which leads them to fight in the hall (or at least make a poor attempt). In detention they declare their hatred for each other. But, in the end, both of them team up to save the class egg project from dying. SpongeBob and Patrick exchange tearful apologies and the episode ends with their friendship restored. Similarly in "The Fry Cook Games," Mr. Krabs and Plankton instigate a spat between SpongeBob and Patrick so they will compete against each other, leading up to a wrestling match. However, SpongeBob and Patrick's anger turns to tears when they realize, by glimpsing their oppositely-colored underwear (pink on SpongeBob, yellow on Patrick), that they do truly care for each other. They exit the arena whistling and holding hands in friendship. Once again, good-temper triumphs over anger and happiness reigns supreme.

There are countless other episodes where a fight between Patrick and SpongeBob, initially caused by anger, is eventually mended by forgiveness and meekness. Staying angry robs SpongeBob of his ultimate goal—to be happy—and seeing Patrick angry doesn't make him happy in the long run; instead, it breaks his spongy heart. This trend to forgive (and, by the next episode, forget) shows that SpongeBob believes in friendship, which is more important than staying angry.

In each of the behaviors examined by Aristotle—courage, honor, truth, and anger—SpongeBob tries to stay on the virtuous path and within the golden mean. It's not a perfect effort, but he makes a good try of it. This is what sets SpongeBob apart from his fellow Bikini Bottom-ites who are defined by their various pursuits of wealth (Mr. Krabs), power (Plankton), praise (Squidward), and listlessness (Patrick). Aristotle actually warns against the pursuit of these—especially in the extreme—since they are not substitutes for real happiness as the result of a virtuous life. SpongeBob, in contrast, is best defined by his desire to pursue a happy life guided by virtuous moderation. In doing so, SpongeBob finds his life assumes a cheerful equilibrium, which is what he is seeking all along.

What Could Be Better than Serving Up Smiles?

Similar to his virtuous characteristics are SpongeBob's attitudes governing his day-to-day routines, from work to relationships. These attitudes, which Aristotle also explores in connection with well-being, include pleasure, wealth, and daily life. Concerning pleasure, the first extreme is hedonism or lack of self-control, while the other is self-denial and forsaking all forms of amusement. Aristotle recognized a virtuous, modest way of how to have fun, which combines simplicity with wisdom and self-control. SpongeBob assumes this stance for the most part as he's not a crazy party animal nor does he believe the best fun in life is no fun at all. His views of pleasure are rather simple and don't involve expensive frills. SpongeBob's favorite hobbies include bubble blowing and jellyfishing (akin to catching butterflies for land-lubbers). He also loves using his imagination, such as in "The Idiot Box" when he and Patrick splurge on a brand new, large-screen television set simply for the giant box it comes in. These methods of entertainment are about as cheap and elementary as they come.

SpongeBob's personal philosophy about fun can actually be summarized in his observations in the "F.U.N. Song":

F is for friends who do stuff together.
U is for you and me.
N is for anywhere and anytime at all—down here in the deep blue sea.

These lyrics "spell out" SpongeBob's virtue-centered ideas about entertainment and pleasure: it should be undertaken with friends and can be had in any place. But there's actually a dash of Aristotle's ideas here. He believed that a truly happy person will acquire friends since friendship is "thought to be the greatest of external goods" (Book IX, Section 9). Friends and companionship are the heart of the "F.U.N. Song" and reflect SpongeBob's views concerning relationships and pleasure. Likewise, use of the words "stuff," "anywhere," and "anytime" indicate a generic tone when it comes to material things. SpongeBob isn't picky about what he and his friends do, where they do it, or when they do it—just as long as it's simple and he can do it with others.

SpongeBob's attitudes towards pleasure and self-satisfaction tie directly into his views about wealth (which includes both money and material possessions). One extreme is stinginess, a hoarder's attitude. Such people never show charity but keep wealth to themselves. The other extreme is wastefulness in which a person gives everything away without prudence.

While SpongeBob is not in need or want of anything materially, he doesn't live high on the hog. In this regard, SpongeBob certainly stands out from his employer, Mr. Krabs, who falls under the stingy category. These characters are a visual parallel between the vice of stinginess and the virtue of charity. For example, in "Patty Hype," SpongeBob opens his own stand to sell "pretty patties" (that is, colored Krabby patties) and ends up making so much money that he gives it away in bags. This upsets Mr. Krabs who reveres wealth above all things, but SpongeBob's focus is finding happiness in making others happy. Likewise, when Mr. Krabs digs a wishing well for the sole purpose of making money, SpongeBob is more concerned with whether or not the wishes are coming true ("Wishing You Well").

When given the task of purchasing Pearl's birthday presents with Mr. Krabs's credit card, SpongeBob cares more about what would bring her the most happiness, not the cost of the gifts. SpongeBob even calls Mr. Krabs out on the carpet for his tightfistedness, calling his employer a "crustaceous cheapskate" when he refuses to rehire Squidward after accusing him of taking Mr. Krabs's first dime ("Can You Spare a Dime?") and "cheapy the cheapskate" when he cons kids into visiting a shoddily built playground all for the sake of making an extra buck ("Krabbyland"). Overall, SpongeBob believes wealth is meant to be shared, such as when he and Patrick argue with Mr. Krabs over who should have the unburied Dutchman's treasure: "One for all!" SpongeBob exclaims to his employer's refrain of "All for one!" ("Arrgh!")

In general, SpongeBob prefers the simple things in life. And, quite frankly, he's not really in tune with opulence. In "Squilliam Returns," Squidward tries to train SpongeBob in the art of fine dining, but all of it seems to perplex poor SpongeBob's brain. Similarly, when SpongeBob breaks his spatula and replaces it with a state-of-the-art, super-deluxe, French-accented model, he finds himself unable to work with it and returns to his old-fashioned, inexpensive spatula ("All that Glitters").

SpongeBob is more comfortable with the simple and inexpensive than the glitz and glitter of elitist culture. But that's not to say he isn't occasionally lured in by the other side. In "Porous Pockets," SpongeBob is tempted by wealth when he cashes in an expensive pearl. This leads to friends of the fancy sort, which leaves simpleton Patrick out of his social circle. However, SpongeBob does not know how to handle his wealth and quickly looses it all. Through it all, he learns that a material-driven life is empty and is brought back to the mean where wealth does not buy friendship or happiness. He is content maintaining a standard of living that relies only on the material necessities he needs to for a quality, happy life.

Just as SpongeBob does not actively try to seek riches, he doesn't hoard what he has either. SpongeBob is willing to open his home for get-togethers and slumber parties with friends and even lets Patrick borrow his possessions, from his prized jellyfishing net, to bath beads, to even a quarter. This also shows how he tries to maintain a moderate lifestyle as SpongeBob is neither overtly driven by wealth nor is he openly stingy with what he has.

It's no mistake SpongeBob prefers to stay at a rather thankless job. Being a fry cook certainly comes with no special benefits other than sweating over a hot, greasy grill for hours on end. SpongeBob, however, remains, not for monetary benefits but because it is what he loves to do and it brings him happiness. Even when tempted to move up, SpongeBob elects to stay. In one instance Jim, Krabs's original fry cook, mentors SpongeBob and asserts "he'll only be great when he finally gets the guts to leave this dump" (The Original Fry Cook"). SpongeBob counters him by declaring the Krusty Krab is not a "dump" and he doesn't intend to seek employment elsewhere. SpongeBob makes a similar decision in "Neptune's Spatula" when he rejects King Neptune's offer for him to serve as the royal fry cook in Atlantis. In this case, SpongeBob opts out of a clearly opulent lifestyle because he sees that not doing so means leaving his friends and the Krusty Krab behind forever, which are the things that matter the most to him and bring him happiness.

All of this adds up to how SpongeBob lives the day-to-day. According to Aristotle, daily life has its extremes, too. The first is living in a state of constant bickering and being quarrelsome. Such persons cannot get along with anyone and, for that reason, lack close relationships. (Plankton, anyone?) On the other side of the coin is flattery where people exist only to please others. But SpongeBob works to keep his daily life in the happy mean. He is gregarious and believes the best in everyone. He strives to avoid arguments and purposely doesn't go around making enemies.

SpongeBob's general outlook on life is governed by optimism and the belief there is a little bit of good in everybody. Even his classic, repetitive catch phrase of "I'm ready!" indicates a willing spirit. On the surface, this could be viewed as naivety, especially when SpongeBob acts kindly towards obvious villains such as Plankton, the occasional bully, and even the Tattletale Strangler. But SpongeBob believes all people should be treated kindly and given a chance to behave rightly. For example, he takes the time to offer "goodness lessons" to Man-Ray, who ends up being "transformed" by SpongeBob's teachings when "the urge to do bad is gone" ("Mermaid Man and Barnacle Boy III"). SpongeBob even tries to give Plankton some pointers in virtue, which don't appear to work out so well since Plankton constantly lives in the extremes of vice without any desire to change. In "Walking Small," SpongeBob's exchange with Plankton, who had talked him into being assertive to scare people away from Goo Lagoon, exposes his recipe for living a virtue-oriented life with a happy end:

> **SpongeBob:** You used me . . . for land development! That wasn't nice.

> **Plankton:** Haven't you figured it out, SpongeBob? Nice guys finish last. Only aggressive people conquer the world.

> **SpongeBob:** Well, . . . what about aggressively nice people?

Afterwards, SpongeBob reclaims the balance of virtue and happiness to, not only the beach patrons, but also his own soul. In his view of life, "aggressively nice people" finish first and strive to make the world a happier place, both for others and themselves.

Why Is It the Best Day Ever?

In a nutshell (or make that a conch shell), SpongeBob isn't an angel, full of goodness and light. But he doesn't actively seek to stay in the darkness of doing bad things. Even SpongeBob realizes his journey to self-mastery is not yet over; he still has rough patches to iron out. "I've got darkness inside of me!" he exclaims, indicating he knows there are sectors of vice within himself ("Night Light"). But just as SpongeBob uses nightlights to banish physical darkness, he equally employs the light of virtue to discard shadows of vice that might steal away his happiness.

Through an application of virtue, whether it's by habit or learned after making a mistake, SpongeBob remains on the path to becoming a self-mastered individual with his sights set on the ultimate goal of a happy life. As Aristotle observed, "the man of Perfected Self-Mastery unites the qualities of Self-Control and Endurance" (Book VII, Section 1). While SpongeBob is far from perfect, he does strive to control his actions and persevere in his practice of virtue.

There's no question SpongeBob does try to live a good life—one that is simple and virtuous. "I am a happy sponge!" he exclaims as he runs around his undersea pineapple home. Aristotle would be proud.

2
The Rule of Dumb?

TIMOTHY DUNN

Patrick Star is not the brightest echinoderm in the sea. In fact, he's downright dim. That may seem a harsh assessment, but it ultimately rings true. Even his parents, whom he often is unable to recognize, think he is "dumber than a sack of diapers" and have to encourage him not to think too hard lest he hurt himself ("I'm with Stupid"). He thinks mayonnaise is a musical instrument ("Band Geeks") and that ice-cream is shiny ("Big Pink Loser").

It's certainly no surprise that Patrick lives under a rock. However, despite his intellectual limitations, he is certainly a lovable character and a loyal friend to SpongeBob. The two are often found frolicking in Jellyfish Fields ("Jellyfishing"), enjoying time together at Glove World ("Rock Bottom"), and spending entire days together using their imagination ("Idiot Box"). When they do fight, they are quick to make-up and see the value in one another and their friendship ("New Student Starfish").

But in the episode "Patrick Smartpants," Patrick's friendship with SpongeBob and his preference for a life of simple pleasures are put to the test. Patrick's faced with a choice between a life filled with simple pleasures and a more dignified and rewarding, though in some respects less pleasurable life. Each life seems worth living, and his choice is not an easy one, no matter how much brain coral is applied to his dilemma.

Patrick SmartPants

The episode begins with a familiar scene: Patrick and SpongeBob laughing raucously while trying, mostly unsuccessfully, to catch jellyfish. Eventually, they decide to play a game of tag. As Patrick sprints gleefully away, he fails to notice the sign warning of a high cliff just ahead. SpongeBob tries to warn him, but Patrick is apparently unable to process the information in time, as he sees the sign, senses something is amiss, but does not slow down. He crashes through the sign and plummets to the sea bottom below. In the resulting impact, Patrick's head is dislodged.

Coming to his aid, SpongeBob re-attaches Patrick's head to his body, unaware that what he thinks is Patrick's head is actually a piece of "brain coral." Patrick's brain is now "plugged in," presumably for the first time. The cobwebs in his head disappear, and the gears start to turn. Instantly Patrick's personality changes and he immediately expresses his distaste for their childish games, calling their laughter "illogical," and expressing admiration for the jellyfish, which he refers to as those "graceful, Stoic creatures of the deep." He quickly finds it difficult to relate to SpongeBob, preferring to "do statistics" or "form hypotheses" about scientific phenomena to jumping rope or running three-legged races.

With a dismayed but persistent SpongeBob in tow, Patrick seeks more intellectually stimulating company. He first pays a call on Squidward, who is busy practicing a difficult piece on the clarinet. At first Squidward is pleasantly surprised when Patrick recognizes the piece he is playing, but Squidward is soon put off by Patrick's condescending tone and overly critical appraisal of Squidward's modest talents. He next visits Sandy Squirrel, who is also initially charmed by his surprisingly sophisticated conversation and wit. But after he solves a difficult math problem that had vexed her, he insults her intelligence, telling her that she "lacks the ability to solve remedial equations." After asking him to leave, she tells him that she "liked him better when he was a barnaclehead."

Unable to find a suitable companion, Patrick tells SpongeBob that they no longer have much in common and must now go their separate ways. But Patrick soon finds the knowledge he has acquired unsatisfying without having a friend with whom to share it. As he looks at a photo album, he vows to do whatever it takes to restore his friendship. In a brilliant montage, we see him try various scientific, technological, and spiritual fixes, but nothing seems to work. He decides at last to enjoy SpongeBob's company, no matter what, by sheer force of will. But alas, he is no longer able to enjoy the games they used to play.

Finally, in an effort to determine its cause, they decide to recreate the events that led to Patrick's remarkable transformation. Eventually they discover both his missing head and the brain coral. Realizing what has happened, SpongeBob asks Patrick if he really wants to "give up being smart." Without hesitation or regret, he declares that "knowledge can never replace friendship. I prefer to be an idiot." Patrick replaces his brain-coral head and instantly becomes his former ignorant, happy self.

We're Just Not Compatible Anymore

Patrick Star is of course a cartoon character, and the dilemma he faces is physically impossible. But the questions raised by this episode are meaningful and deeply relevant to our own lives. Did Patrick make the right choice? How do we compare the life of a happy ignoramus to that of a discontented genius? Which is the better life? Did Patrick make a heroic sacrifice for the sake of a deep and meaningful friendship? Or did he squander an opportunity not only to acquire wisdom and knowledge, but also to build deeper, more satisfying relationships with others? Should we strive to improve our own intellectual capacities, or are we, too, better off being dumb?

Before we examine how philosophers might answer these questions, it's helpful to consider briefly why anyone might think that Patrick made the right decision. There are at least two ways of defending Patrick's decision to revert to the life of a happy idiot. The first argument relies on a subjectivist account of value. Subjectivists hold that there's no such thing as an objective good or value; rather, what is good or bad is determined by each individual. Whatever a person believes is good is good for that person (though not necessarily for others).

According to this subjectivist view, it's impossible to rationally criticize another person's values, or compare one person's value choices to another's. I might prefer to develop my talents and spend time having good conversations, but if someone does not share these values, I have no basis for saying that she is wrong or mistaken. Her choices are just different—right for her, wrong for me. If Patrick believes that he's better off being dumb, then who are we to say that he made the wrong choice?

A slightly different way to defend Patrick's decision is to say that while some choices are objectively better than others, and thus subject to rational criticism, Patrick would in fact be happier being ignorant. Patrick made the right choice because objectively, what matters most is being happy, and at least for Patrick, being an ignoramus and thereby restoring his friendship with SpongeBob is the best route to happiness. This view leaves it an open question whether making an analogous decision would be the right thing for us to do.

Perhaps you or I would not be happy spending much of the day chasing jellyfish or engaging in snail racing. But if these activities make a person happy, then he or she ought to pursue them. Notice that this view also implies that a person can make the wrong decision or have the wrong values. Suppose that out of a sense of moral obligation, or pretentious intellectual snobbery (Squidward anyone?), I spend the day engaging in interpretive dance or playing in a clarinet trio in the park, but these activities leave me bored and unfulfilled. Then according to this view, I ought to do something else. Happiness itself is an objective good, but what makes a person happy will depend, at least in part, on the individual.

Let Us Go Off and Admire the Beauty and Fragility of Nature

Patrick Star decides that a life devoted to the pursuit of pleasure is preferable to a life devoted to intellectual pursuits that left him feeling isolated and lonely. While one might expect philosophers to decry his choice outright, Patrick's difficult decision might actually find some sympathy in the writings of John Stuart Mill (1806–1873), a British philosopher who is one of the most eloquent expositors and defenders of the theory of hedonistic utilitarianism.[1]

Hedonistic utilitarians hold that the right action is the one that maximizes happiness for all. Happiness, in turn, is defined as "pleasure and the absence of pain." Thus the

---

[1] John Stuart Mill, *Utilitarianism* (Hackett, 2001).

right action is the one that maximizes the net balance of pleasure and pain for all.[2] Furthermore, pleasure is the only thing intrinsically good—good in and of itself, for its own sake. All other goods are good only insofar as they promote pleasure or minimize pain. Health, wealth, and knowledge, for example, are commonly thought of as goods, but their goodness lies in their ability to increase pleasure or minimize pain. They are not in themselves good or bad.

We might think that hedonistic utilitarians would look favorably on Patrick's decision. After all, if pleasure is the only thing good in itself, and Patrick takes more pleasure in the life of a happy simpleton, then isn't he better off being dumb? Responding to this kind of argument (which Mill's critics regarded as evidence of the absurdity of utilitarianism), Mill distinguishes between two types of pleasure: higher and lower. Higher pleasures are, roughly, the pleasures of the mind and include such things as knowledge, wisdom, and understanding; aesthetic experience; moral sentiments such as sympathy, compassion, and justice; love and affection; and many others as well. Lower pleasures are, roughly, physical or bodily pleasures, such as the pleasures of eating and drinking.

Mill does not define these categories very precisely, preferring instead to give a few examples of pleasures in each category. And it's not clear that they can be defined very precisely, as many pleasures seem to belong in both categories. The pleasure of enjoying a carefully prepared meal, for example, seems to involve both physical and

---

[2] Mill defines right actions somewhat differently. For Mill, "actions are right in proportion as they tend to promote happiness; wrong as they tend to promote the reverse of happiness" (*Utilitarianism*, p. 7). This has logical consequences that differ from the maximization formulation above, but the latter formulation is commonly accepted, and in any case this chapter is not directly concerned with Mill's conception of the right action but rather with his conception of the good.

mental pleasures, as do many other examples. Still, this is not a fatal problem for Mill, as there are many examples that obviously fit into one category or another, and this is enough for our purposes.

For Mill, the distinction between higher and lower pleasures is not merely a quantitative distinction. That is, higher pleasures are not higher merely because they are generally less costly, more permanent, or are accompanied with fewer side effects (reading Shakespeare, for example, is cheaper than a night of binging on Triple Goober Berry Sunrises and is less likely to result in hangovers and embarrassing memories). Rather, they are also qualitatively superior, by which he means superior in kind and not merely in degree.

For many of us, this claim may seem a bit strange. How do we determine whether one pleasure or type of pleasure is superior in kind to another? Does this even make sense? Anticipating this potential objection, Mill attempts to defend his view by appealing to the Doctrine of Competent Judges:

> Of two pleasures, if there be one to which all or almost all who have experience of both give a decided preference, irrespective of any feeling of moral obligation to prefer it, that is the more desirable pleasure. If one of the two is, by those who are competently acquainted with both, placed so far above the other that they prefer it, even though knowing it to be attended with a greater amount of discontent, and would not resign it for any quantity of the other pleasure which their nature is capable of, we are justified in ascribing to the preferred enjoyment a superiority in quality so far outweighing quantity as to render it, in comparison, of small account. (*Utilitarianism*, pp. 8–9)

In other words, only those who have experienced both types of pleasure are capable of deciding which of two types of pleasure is superior. For example, the experience of watching a movie that engages my imagination, forces me to challenge my beliefs or reflect on my values, provokes complex emotional reactions, and so on, is qualitatively superior to that of a dull, predictable, formulaic, unimaginative action movie or romantic comedy. It is superior, that is, if those who have seen both, or at least have had both types of experience, judge it to be superior. Those who have experienced only one type of pleasure are not competent to determine which of the two is preferable. And if there is disagreement among competent judges, the majority opinion is the final arbiter of value.

Accordingly, the fact that a person prefers blowing bubbles to karate does not entail that blowing bubbles is superior in quality to karate—the person who prefers bubble blowing might simply be incompetent, or perhaps overruled by a majority of other competent judges.

As to what types of pleasure competent judges deem superior, Mill claims that

it is an unquestionable fact that those who are equally acquainted with and equally capable of appreciating and enjoying both do give a most marked preference to the manner of existence which employs their higher faculties . . . no intelligent human being would consent to be a fool, no instructed person would be an ignoramus, no person of feeling and conscience would be selfish and base, even though they should be persuaded that the fool, the dunce, or the rascal is better satisfied with his lot than they are with theirs. (p. 9)

Mill is usually an extremely clear writer, but in his discussion of higher and lower pleasures he does not always clearly distinguish pleasure as a conscious mental state from pleasure as a capacity, or rather, the capacity for pleasure. A person might have the capacity for pleasure without actually experiencing pleasure. Squidward and Plankton, for example, are rarely seen taking any pleasure out of life, but each still has the capacity to experience such feelings. This is true even if we are simply talking about lower pleasures. A person with a very refined palate, for instance, has a capacity for intense gustatory pleasures, but if he or she is eating a ketchup, onion, and peanut plant sundae ("Something Smells") this capacity will largely remain unengaged. For our purposes, it is best to interpret Mill's claim as primarily about the capacity for pleasure. This is evident from his famous claim that "it is better to be Socrates dissatisfied than a fool satisfied" (p. 10). That Socrates does not experience much pleasure is less important; what matters is that he retain the capacity for higher pleasures.

Understanding pleasure as a capacity, we are now in a position to see why Mill would say that Patrick made a terrible mistake. Once transformed, Patrick went from being a dull ignoramus to being a sophisticated, cultivated genius. He was no longer able to enjoy the primitive pleasures that SpongeBob enjoys (playing jump rope, having one legged races, engaging in a round of duck-duck-hermit-crab, or "belch-talking"), but found satisfaction only in endeavors that challenged his rather advanced abilities (thus, the math problem that puzzled Sandy was, for him, a rather dull exercise). To be sure, he eventually became alienated from others, but this was not merely a result of his greater capacities—he also treated others with condescension, priggishness, and snobbery.

Mill is of course not saying that a capacity for superior pleasures makes one a morally superior person. Patrick likely could have experienced a great deal of higher pleasure making friends with both his intellectual equals, and others of more modest abilities, had he chosen to do so. That he opted to forgo these higher pleasures, in favor of a life of lower pleasures, implies that he settled for a life capable of less overall happiness.

As for the arguments sketched above, Mill plainly rejects the subjectivist's view of the good. For Mill, some pleasures just are better than others, qualitatively. Reading poetry simply is better than playing children's games, at least to adults (who presumably have experience of both, while children know only one side of the story). Patrick SmartPants certainly thought so, until he changed his mind. And for Mill, since happiness is just pleasure and the absence of pain, to be happy a person ought to seek and develop her capacities for higher pleasures. Since Patrick essentially destroyed these capacities, Mill, although generally sympathetic to Patrick's preference for a life of pleasure, would conclude that our pink friend acted foolishly.

When Did the Fun Go Away, SpongeBob?

But perhaps the super intelligent Patrick Star considered Mill's position. What objections might overrule Mill's otherwise negative assessment of Patrick's choice? I want to consider possible objections to Mill's account just as Patrick might have done. To understand the first objection, it is important to distinguish between two claims: 1. There is a qualitative distinction between higher and lower pleasures, and only those who have experienced both are competent to decide which of two pleasures is higher; 2. In the real world, those who have experienced both in fact prefer the kinds of pleasures that Mill considers to be higher; or, put another way, people generally prefer to develop and seek the satisfaction of the capacities that Mill considers to be higher.

Notice that these two claims are logically distinct. The first is a philosophical claim about what makes something a higher pleasure, while the second is an empirical claim about what types of pleasures people actually prefer. Accordingly, one can accept the first claim without accepting the second. And this might seem to be a plausible position. For even if we suppose that #1 is true, why does Mill think that most or even a majority of competent judges consistently prefer the pleasures that he considers to be inferior?

Although consumer preferences are an imperfect guide to people's "true" preferences, doesn't the fact that the fast food, tobacco, and liquor industries are thriving indicate what types of pleasure ordinary people seek, at least in the US? In response to this objection, Mill argues that social conditions, such as poverty or a laborious job, make it difficult for a person to retain his desire to develop his higher faculties; unless constantly nourished, such a desire can easily fade away. For SpongeBob and Patrick, it may be difficult for an overworked and under-paid fry cook and his unemployed friend to develop these higher faculties. Moreover, Mill asserts that people

> lose their high aspirations as they lose their intellectual tastes, because they have not time or opportunity for indulging them; and they addict themselves to inferior pleasures, not because they deliberately prefer them, but because they are either the only ones to which they have access or the only ones which they are any longer capable of enjoying. (pp. 10–11)

Is Mill's response sufficient to handle this objection? I can think of at least two worries one might still have.

First, do social and psychological pressures really explain why so many people seem to prefer lower pleasures to higher ones? Why not simply accept people's actual preferences at face value? Perhaps they prefer lower pleasures because, having experienced both, they find lower pleasures to be more satisfying. If we look at people's actual preferences, it might be more accurate to say that people prefer a life that combines a healthy amount of both higher and lower pleasures. Mill's dismissal of the preferences that people seem actually to have could be construed as snobby or elitist. To that position we might tell Mill, "Don't be a Squidward."

Second, to insist that psychological and social pressures explain away people's actual preferences is itself a claim for which Mill provides little evidence. Before we can evaluate this claim, we need to know under what conditions it would be falsified. For example, if a person insisted that she preferred a Krabby Patty to Filet Mignon, not for social or psychological reasons but just because she prefers its taste, then why shouldn't we accept her word, instead of assuming that her preferences have been socially determined? If Mill were to insist that, no matter what a person says, her preference for lower pleasures is socially determined and therefore somehow illegitimate, he would be dogmatically insulating his view from possible empirical refutation.

Another objection relies on the distinction between the experience of pleasure and the capacity for pleasure. If a person with higher faculties consistently and repeatedly experiences few such pleasures, what good is the capacity? The mere possibility of experiencing higher forms of pleasure is, at least for hedonistic utilitarians, not as important as the actual experience of pleasure. This objection reveals a tension, if not an inconsistency, in Mill's account. To the extent that we value the actual experience of pleasure, the mere capacity for higher pleasures loses some of its value.

A very dissatisfied Socrates (or Sheldon Plankton, for that matter) might actually be less happy than a very happy fool (our delightfully cheerful Mr. SquarePants), even if the latter is capable of experiencing only lower forms of pleasure. If Mill responds that this fails to take seriously the claim that higher pleasures are qualitatively superior, and that accordingly no amount of lower pleasure can outweigh any amount of higher pleasure, then we're entitled to press the first objection all the more forcefully. Such a view seems to fly in the face of the choices that competent judges actually make. On the other hand, if Mill insists that it's the capacity for higher pleasure that matters most, then it's unclear how he can also claim that pleasure and the absence of pain (understood as an experience) is the only thing good in and of itself.

How Can I Compete with Geniusness?

Most contemporary utilitarians do not rely on Mill's distinction between higher and lower pleasures. Instead, they would insist that higher capacities are valuable because, in most cases at least, such capacities do in fact produce quantitatively more pleasurable lives for those who have them. Perhaps a Patrick SmartPants very dissatisfied would be less happy than a very satisfied fool (Patrick any other time), but such cases are rare and we would do well not to seek satisfaction only in "lower" pleasures. Accordingly, even if there is no qualitative distinction between types of pleasures, we still have reason to question Patrick's decision. As happy as the life of a simpleton might be, the possibility of more lasting, satisfying, and fulfilling pleasures more than makes up for the greater dissatisfaction that often attends the life of the mind.

3
The Artistic Genius of the Miserable Squidward

NATASHA NOEL LIEBIG

He lives in a stone statue under the sea. Grey, and moody, and grumpy is he. He works as a cashier at the Krusty Krab, but grumbles a lot and hates his job. He thinks SpongeBob and Patrick are idiots. He is an intolerant narcissist, but is always unfortunate. He refers to himself as a genius, and Squilliam Fancyson is his nemesis.

Squidward Quincy Tentacles, a grey-green walking octopus (not a squid as is commonly assumed because of his name), is the grumpy next-door neighbor of SpongeBob. His character is juxtaposed with SpongeBob and Patrick who are goofy, lighthearted, easily gratified, and have the imagination of a child. Squidward is often disgusted by the antics of his neighbors, particularly SpongeBob. He finds them to be intolerable, even though they think of him as a friend.

Everything about Squidward is gloomy, miserable, and serious; even his appearance illustrates a glum, pessimistic image of the world. His color is a depressive grey-green, he is bald, his nose and tentacles droop, he has a constant frown, his eyelids sag, and he grumbles in a low, flat voice. Squidward's house is a stone statue in the form of the Easter Island stone heads. His house embodies his austere, sober nature. It is dark grey, dull, lifeless, lacking any vibrancy or color, unlike SpongeBob's house that is a bright, cheery pineapple.

Squidward is perpetually unhappy and feels sorry for himself. He's always trying to impress and beat his rival Squilliam, of whom he is jealous, but to no avail. He ignores others and *will* laugh at their pain. He really wants to be famous and dreams of having a full head of hair. He reads luxury magazines because he vainly desires to have a fancier, more lucrative life of luxury and peace. Yet, he is marred by failure and is quite unfortunate.

Philosophy has its own Squidward, actually. His name is Arthur Schopenhauer and he lived in Germany in the late-eighteenth and nineteenth centuries. Schopenhauer's brand of pessimist philosophy suggests that Squidward's unhappiness comes from the nature of the world and because life is basically a miserable, futile struggle.

Breaking new ground in the philosophic tradition by introducing the concept of embodiment in terms of how we engage with the world, Schopenhauer is well-known for elevating art and emphasizing the importance of art as a way to temporarily escape the miserable existence that life is. If we look to his main work, *The World as Will and Representation*, we can see how Squidward's character exemplifies this philosophy through his demeanor, appearance, activities, and the nature of his role in the show.[1]

The World as Squilliam and Idea

Squidward's bleak outlook on life is reflected in Schopenhauer's pessimist perspective, which suggests that life is not only miserable, but meaningless. Schopenhauer

---

[1] Arthur Schopenhauer, *The World as Will and Representation, In Two Volumes* (New York: Dover, 1966).

sees our actions and aims as futile, suggesting we have no mastery over the nature of the world, or even ourselves. Perhaps this is why Squidward often feels as though he is a victim of circumstance, struggling at a job he doesn't like and suffering the indignities of others. Such suffering comes from the world's inner-most nature, which is the "*will*-to-live."

Schopenhauer holds that everything "presses" or "pushes" itself into existence, and the highest form of existence is organic existence, *life*.[2] He argues that there is a universal craving for life, and that this craving and *will*-to-live is the only eternal and unconditioned quality about nature. The *will*-to-live continuously grasps at whatever it can to satisfy this craving and thus "presses impetuously into existence" in a multitude of various forms, conditions, and locations. Humans are one of those forms. This means that each of us is to be understood as nothing more than manifestations of this *will*-to-live, and are no more valuable or significant than animal (or sea creature) life.

Schopenhauer's pessimistic perspective on life is further developed into his conception of what he calls the *will*. According to Schopenhauer, there is an innermost nature of the world that drives, determines, and motivates our actions and all observable phenomena. Individuals are motivated by basic needs and their own desires which are an expression of this *will*. The *will* is a metaphysical existence, that is, what we would think of as "reality." Squidward, like any one of us according to Schopenhauer, is nothing other than embodied *will*, a being who persistently desires and needs without any conscious reflection or control.

---

[2] *The World as Will and Representation*, Volume II, p. 350.

Desire, then, is the condition for suffering and distress because we lack what is desired and struggle to obtain it. Much as Squidward's perpetual pining for musical notoriety or recognition for his artistic genius causes him great distress given the disappointing reality of his everyday life, if we do not obtain what we desire the stress continues. Yet, desire is futile, illogical, directionless, even though it is the source of all action in the world. This creates the conditions of eternal frustration in individuals the same as expressed in the bitter condescension with which Squidward lashes out and mistreats others, while also desperately seeking their praise. Schopenhauer might describe Squidward and the rest of us as "constantly needy creatures who continue for a time merely by devouring one another, pass their existence in anxiety and want, and often endure terrible afflictions, until they fall at last into the arms of death" (p. 349).

Schopenhauer believes that it doesn't matter what we desire out of life. Desire is simply a fundamental aspect of the *will* and that we continue to struggle to fulfill our wants until we die. Even if Squidward were to fulfill his dreams of being a famous clarinetist—more famous even than the wealthy and admired Squilliam Fancyson—he would still not be content. His *will* would form in him further desires that drive him and cause him to suffer more and more as those desires increase. And though this causes him to endure perpetual misery, it's a force over which he has no control. The tendency to maintain life and continue it as long as possible is independent of all knowledge. This means that the *will* does not come about through some type of conscious, rational, intelligible process of decision. Rather, the *will*-to-live is an impulse, a blind urge. It exists without either foundation or purpose.

It is for this reason that according to Schopenhauer, the *will* is prior to our intellect. The *will* does not have an intellectual characteristic, but instead drives the intellect. This means that desire, as the *will*, is prior to thought. Yet, it is an aimless, non-rational urge, endless striving, and devoid of knowledge.

In a sense, then, Squidward is really striving for no reason at all. Since his *will* is a non-rational, aimless struggle to satisfy an insatiable desire, his world under the sea has no discernible purpose. No wonder he's so miserable all the time. Such a grim image of life, trying to manufacture meaning where there is none, is a bitter way to live.

Who Are You Calling Big Nose, Big Nose?

Schopenhauer's philosophy does suggest that we can come to know of this innermost character of nature, or the thing-in-itself, through our own subjective experience of our bodies. We experience our bodies in two ways: First, there is an objective relation in the sense that we have an idea of the body, which is how we experience all other objects in the world. Second, we experience our bodies through an immediate, distinct manifestation of our internal perception through how our bodies operate in the world. This is best recognized through the concept of motivation.

When Squidward has an intention to perform a certain action, such as painting numerous self-portraits or playing "music," he becomes aware of his body in an unmediated way through an internal awareness of the movement required to perform that action. This is only experienced by him performing the action. However, he also has an objective knowledge of this motivation by watching his body move, and others in Bikini Bottom can witness his movement, thus creating an Idea or representation of the body.

Squidward's subjective experience of his *will*, however, is not experienced through spatial, temporal, or casual apprehension. It is a self-determined, blind impulse or urges that are not driven by any rational trajectory, as suggested above. Since the *will* is what drives motions and actions, his *will* is the cause of his experience and he is subject to it. Yet, he cannot help but structure his experience of his bodily movements through objective configurations of space and time, cause and effect. Although, when it comes down to it, our only way of really knowing or experiencing this *will* is through our own subjective, embodied feelings, sensations, emotions, and perceptions, rather than through objective concepts of space, time, and cause and effect.

Consequently, we, like Squidward, can come into contact and understanding with the nature of the world by coming into contact and understanding with ourselves. There's a distinction between the person, the self, or the "subject," and the objects of the world. This distinction, according to Schopenhauer, is the general condition for human knowledge. Our knowledge of the world is derived from our relationship to our bodies. Likewise, other external objects, like SpongeBob's pineapple, also have both representations and have a particular internal characteristic of their own. The *will* is objectified into a set of universal objects, that is, Ideas. The Idea is the basis of all relations and is a complete, objective phenomenon.

Such qualities as colors and other features are immediately apprehended and provide for the apprehension of the Idea through perception, but they do not belong to the Idea. That is, we can apprehend that a jellyfish is pink, but this quality of pink does not belong to the Idea of the jellyfish. Rather, the Idea is just a medium of expression. Accordingly, there is a world of the *will* in itself, and a world of representations. Yet, the *will* and representations are one and the same reality but seen from different perspectives.

Therefore, we do have some insight into the nature of the world through our own innermost nature, that is, a manifestation of the *will*. But Schopenhauer's picture of the world also implies that we do not have "free will." We are determined through the *will*, such as how our actions, motivations, and thoughts are driven by the *will*. Ultimately, though, life is a series of misfortunes and accidents that is indifferent to us. If we feel free, it's only in the sense that we cognitively structure our actions through the principle of cause and effect.

I feel the experience of freedom of action because I believe that I caused myself to do such an action. Yet, what's lying behind the apparent freedom to do such an action is the blind, irrational *will* which all of our actions are subject to. Squidward believes he has the freedom to create a better life, but as we see, he cannot get there, despite his struggles. In any circumstance he has at obtaining something, even peace and tranquility, this is countered by others, such as Squilliam Fancyson and SpongeBob.

Where Happiness Is Just a Suction Cup Away

Squidward's potential happiness is also frustrated in another way. Any desire that he has that is satisfied is often gained at the expense of others. This amounts to *bellum omnium*; a perpetual state of struggle with others. SpongeBob and Patrick play away, blindly seeking their own pleasure and fun, but in doing so they interrupt and frustrate Squidward's plans at success or tranquility. The roots of their joy cause his unhappiness. This is what also makes happiness unobtainable. It would require that other people's desires not be in conflict with our own. We cannot seek out and obtain the object of our desire without disrupting the *will* of the other. Therefore, Schopenhauer argues that the *will* to life is necessarily, grimly aggressive. In a sense, the *will* turns in on itself and does violence to itself.

Our unhappiness, though, does not arise from some sort of event, like being stung by a jellyfish, but is always already present in mere existence. And in this sense, there is nothing that we can do to alleviate the pain we experience. However, from looking at all the animals and ourselves aspire so restlessly, we cannot help but look for some type of aim or purpose for it all. We desire that life be valuable, that it have a purpose, and be meaningful. Yet, in this way, we impart value to our lives, and so we above anything else love a life that really is nothing but miserable, painful, aggressive struggle.

It is not that life is some wonderful, desirable, pleasurable thing to be valued, which gives us a reason, some meaningful purpose, for living. Nope, we continue to struggle to live, despite how miserable it is because that is the nature of the world. If we really thought about this and considered it objectively, Schopenhauer notes, we would abhor it. And in this sense, life is comical. Despite how serious our care, desire, or worry may be, we're often frustrated only to be embarrassed (as Squidward often is) and this shows how ridiculous such struggle is.

If we consider all of this: that the *will-to-live* is necessarily greedy desire and need that perpetually frustrates us, the *will* is indifferent to us, our desires, and happiness, our aims are pointless because they cannot be achieved, ultimately our lives are meaningless, and that the *will* is necessarily seeking to fulfill its desire always at the cost of the other—this makes for such a miserable existence that Schopenhauer suggests that the world really should not exist at all.

I Listen to Public Radio

Yet, there is a subtle bit of optimism in Schopenhauer's philosophy, and this can be seen in how Squidward finds short moments of happiness and relaxation. Squidward is an artist—he likes interpretive dance and sculpture, paints pictures of himself, and plays the clarinet, though not very well. It is through art that he escapes the struggle and miserable existence in fleeting moments of peace, that is, until SpongeBob and Patrick come along and interrupt his peace.

These fleeting moments of happiness can be accounted for by what Schopenhauer believes to be the artistic perspective in life. As he says, "Life is *never* beautiful, but only the pictures of it, namely in the transfiguring of art or of poetry, particularly in youth, when we do not yet know it" (p. 374). When we have an aesthetic way of thinking about the world, we recognize the way in which the world is just that—Ideas, and these ideas are outside of time, space, and causality. It is through these representations, these objective Ideas that we strip the *will*-full element of life.

The introduction of an Idea to us is based on a change in us, and as Schopenhauer notes, it is in a sense, self-denial. We deny the existence of the driving, blind, impulsive, irrational *will* in the transition to purely objective knowledge. This change is required for the work of art. Art, including fine arts, music, architecture, painting, poetry, sculpture, visual and literary arts, correspond to the world of representation in immediate objectification. To paint a sunset is an immediate objectification of a sunset, an Idea, in which our own individual *will* is stripped out. In other words, in painting the sunset, the sunset is an object and we are engaging with the world through this objective, aesthetic perspective.

It's little wonder Squidward spends so much time painting himself! Further, to have the Idea of a sunset does not depend on our individual *will.* When the objects are universal Ideas, then the subject of experience becomes universal aesthetic perception which thus raises a person into a pure *will*-less, painless, subject of knowledge. The more conscious of the Idea, the less conscious of our own subjective nature we are. We perceive the world objectively only when we no longer perceive that we do not belong to it, that is, that the world *is* Idea.

It's only when we have no interest in the Ideas that we experience this temporary transcendence of the *will* through apprehending the pure objective nature of things. The separation of the *will* through objectification, aesthetic perception, is a way to do this. Aesthetic contemplation is a way to separate the person from the miserable world by objectifying that world through the Idea, in which they somehow negate the *will* and do not *will* at all. We lose ourselves in the object and forget about our individuality. In this way, we transcend the subjective way of seeing or apprehending the object. The world is objectified through the manifestation of the nature itself.

Music is particularly a way to do this. Squidward plays the clarinet and appears to be happy in this moment. He is lost, you could say, in the music and is not in the presence of, or aware of, his miserable existence. Music for Schopenhauer is the most metaphysical art in that it duplicates the basic structure of the world as a whole. Music embodies abstract forms of feelings—sadness itself, joy itself, without contingent contents that would typically cause suffering. It is an expression of emotion in a detached and disinterested way which allows apprehension of the nature of the world without frustration involved in daily life. Thus, when Squidward plays the clarinet, he does not have some sort of futile struggle in the world which causes him pain and suffering.

However, according to Schopenhauer, few people can do this. It is just the artistically-minded genius who contemplates these Ideas and creates a work of art that portrays them in a manner more clear and accessible. The artistic genius communicates universalistic vision to those who lack it. The highest purpose of art is, just this, to communicate platonic ideas. According to Schopenhauer, the mark of the genius is that he is always sees the universal in the particular, that is, he sees the Idea of the sunset in the sunset. On the other hand, the normal person is caught up with life and is only interested in things and events of his life, not their objective significance. For a genius, his poetry painting, and other works of art are an end in itself, whereas for most people, they desire such things for their own interest. But, as Schopenhauer argues, it is the genius who is great because he does not seek his own interests but pursues only an objective end.

Schopenhauer likens the genius to the child. According to Schopenhauer, the genius has a childlike character in terms of the need of the *imagination* to "complete, arrange, amplify, fix, retain, and repeat at pleasure all the significant pictures of life" to communicate that Idea. But also, the genius must be child-like in order that his perception is not tied to the real presence of things, as in the material world. As Schopenhauer says, "every genius is already a big child, since he looks out into the world as into something strange and foreign, a drama, and thus with purely objective interest" (p. 395). A child looks at the world in wonder without any subjective desire and *will* to master it, so too does the genius.

It is funny to think about Squidward as having a child-like manner. If he is a genius after all, then according to Schopenhauer, he would have that child-like element, in other words, he would have to be more like SpongeBob and Patrick. The question is, then, who is more of a genius—Squidward or SpongeBob? SpongeBob certainly seems to be able to transcend the miserable conditions of life, whereas for Squidward, it is only in temporary moments that he does so. Yet, Squidward does so through art.

Likewise, according to Schopenhauer, any such moment of respite from the world through art is only a small break in misery, an absence of pain and struggle. This is because our corporality, our embodied nature, interrupts this temporary suspension of the self and brings us back to the discomforting, miserable life: emotions, hunger, cares, greedy desire always interrupt such moments. We are nothing other than the *will* embodied, after all. Yet, it is because this happiness is momentary that it keeps us perpetually in a state of desire.

The momentary satisfaction is what keeps us continuing to strive for satisfying our desires. Once the moment has passed, we continue to desire to be released from the miserable struggle and obtain happiness again. If we were to obtain what we desired permanently, if we could maintain a state of aesthetic perception, the *will*-less state would continue and our desire would cease. But this doesn't happen and we are always looking into the future to plan for our happiness, just like Squidward reading his luxury magazines, looking ahead to where he could some day transcend his miserable life of living next to SpongeBob, working at the Krusty Krab.

Maybe this is why we need such cartoons as SpongeBob SquarePants, if life is how Schopenhauer portrays it to be. It seems as though if Schopenhauer were to create a character, it would be Squidward. Yet, despite what it may seem Squidward is actually a very fun character. His distaste and annoyance of SpongeBob and Patrick create a tension in the show that allows for comedic situations. Without the grouchy Squidward, SpongeBob and Patrick would not seem as ridiculous and silly as they do. And we are often able to laugh, as Squidward does at others, at Squidward's failures and frustrations, if only to escape our own miserable struggle in the world for a little while. This perhaps is the genius of Squidward's character.

4

Eugene Krabs and the True Value of a Dollar

JOSEPH J. FOY

In "Krusty Love," Mr. Krabs sits cheerfully singing behind the desk in his office as he cross-stitches the image of a dollar bill. Suddenly, he smells that there is something wrong with the cash register. He rushes to it and after a quick sniff and shake realizes that there is only forty-nine dollars and eight cents in the drawer—a penny short!

Squidward condescendingly dismisses the crying Krabs's woes, and when SpongeBob tries to console his boss by telling him that "it's just a penny, sir, it doesn't matter," Krabs becomes outraged. He shouts at SpongeBob: "Doesn't matter? It's money that makes the world go 'round, boy. It's money that keeps your pants square. It's money that keeps Squidward in fancy soap. It's money that paid for all them renovations we did. Oh, nothing in all the seven seas could matter more."

Despite his immediate claim to the contrary, Krabs does find something in the seven seas that matters as much—the "curvy-cutie," Mrs. Puff. After using SpongeBob to awkwardly court her, Krabs gets a date with the boating instructor and spends the entire time smitten by her while simultaneously ruing how much money the date is costing him. The time Krabs and Puff spend together is disastrous because of the crustacean's obsession over money and material goods, which comes at the expense of them developing any meaningful attachment or connection (and is absolute torture on SpongeBob, who is commanded to go buy things for Mrs. Puff by his employer, and then is verbally berated for spending all of Mr. Krabs's money).

How might we evaluate the character of Mr. Eugene Harold Krabs? Is he to be praised for his entrepreneurial success and money-making abilities? Is he to be condemned for his mistreatment and exploitative oppression of his employees (not to mention his customers)? Or does Mr. Krabs suffer from a moral failing that is all too familiar to the unexamined life?

What a Money-Tastical Day

To begin, it is important that we evaluate Mr. Krabs's admirable qualities. If Krabs had no respectable traits, we might view him no differently than that nefarious little microorganism, Sheldon J. Plankton. After all, Mr. Krabs possesses the intellect and creativity that led to the development of the well-guarded secret formula for producing Bikini Bottom's best-loved sandwich, the Krabby Patty (a sandwich so wonderful that SpongeBob suggests that it's "good for your soul"). Likewise, it is through his continued management efforts to produce a quality product and establishment that the Krusty Krab stays (metaphorically, anyway) afloat. In fact, one might argue that those traits that are sometimes critiqued in Krabs—his selfishness, his seemingly singular obsession with money, and being cheap—are not really vices because they open the doors to his continued success.

In one of her best-known works, *Atlas Shrugged*, Ayn Rand (1905–1982), a novelist whose writings have inspired numerous essays and examinations of philosophical objectivism, uses the character Francisco d'Anconia to articulate how the value of money goes far beyond its mere rate of exchange.[1] Through d'Anconia, Rand suggests that money is the result of production, which itself stems from intellectual effort, labor, and moral fortitude. Similar to Mr. Krabs's lecture to SpongeBob on the value of money, Rand begins d'Anconia's speech:

> "Have you ever asked what is the root of money? Money is a tool of exchange, which can't exist unless there are goods produced and men able to produce them. Money is the material shape of the principle that men who wish to deal with one another must deal by trade and give value for value. Money is not the tool of the moochers, who claim your product by tears, or of the looters, who take it from you by force. Money is made possible only by the men who produce. Is this what you consider evil?" (*Atlas Shrugged*, p. 381)

Rand goes on to discuss the value of money in representational terms—that which money signifies and its usefulness in achieving other things. As d'Anconia suggests, "money is only a tool. It will take you wherever you wish, but it will not replace you as the driver. It will give you the means for the satisfaction of your desires, but it will not provide you with desires" (p. 382). To that end, Rand, like Krabs, holds the view that, far from being at the heart of evil, "money is the root of all good."

Superficially, Rand glorifies individuals like Krabs who unapologetically live their lives in pursuit of their own interests. She suggests that systems that attempt to promote general equality and restrict an individual's ability to pursue wealth for their own use, often those systems that use taxation to redistribute wealth to the less privileged,

---

[1] Ayn Rand, *Atlas Shrugged* (Penguin, 1999).

destroy creativity and stifle greatness to the point that nothing better than mediocrity survives. From Rand's perspective, we should not only praise Krabs, we should attempt to be more like him.

To be fair to Rand, it's unclear that she would universally commend all of Krabs's moneymaking schemes. In fact, she has d'Anconia describe how money is made and kept by the ambitious and intelligent person, whereas the lazy and ignorant person would never make a fortune (or would foolishly squander away one that was inherited). However, because their actions are—indirectly at least—judged collectively in the pursuits of individuals in an open market place, we can at least assume that Rand would extol the ability of Krabs to make money over the likes of Plankton. Even if Krabs may engage in some questionable practices, overall we might conclude from Rand's perspective that he is to be praised for offering a product to meet the demands of his patrons. The Krusty Krab produces superior profits, and the market has spoken.

Krabby the Clown or Cheapy the Cheapskate?

To assume that the bottom-line of revenue generation is the end of the story, however, is to replace questions about morality and ethics with answers of profit and money-making. Krabs's pursuit of money is not entirely praiseworthy. For example, in "Wishing You Well," Krabs attempts to profit himself by taking advantage of the belief that throwing money in a well will grant your sincerest wish, while in "Krabby Land," Mr. Krabs even attempts to bilk children out of their money. In the eco-conscious short "The Endless Summer," Krabs intentionally engages in polluting the atmosphere, harming the environment and the collective goods that are open to all, so that he can make more money off of his newly opened swimming pool, while in "Jellyfish Hunter" he almost destroys the population of jellyfish in Jellyfish Fields in attempting to harvest them for a new Krabby Patty sauce. Perhaps most flagrant of all, he's willing to endanger the health and safety of his customers in order to make a quick buck, even when he has full knowledge that he is about to sell a defective product ("Born Again Krabs").

In addition to the harm he imposes on the community at-large, and the way he treats his customers, Krabs all but physically abuses his employees. He forces them to at times work twenty-three and twenty-four hours a day while paying them very little. In "Fear of a Krabby Patty," Krabs forces SpongeBob to provide forty three days of non-stop, twenty-four-hour service until the fry cook finally snaps and develops a neurotic fear of Krabby Patties. Likewise, in the episodes "Squeaky Boots" and "Skill Crane," Krabs is shown paying his employees in cash, presumably to avoid the tax liabilities and labor regulations of reporting his payroll. In "Squid on Strike," he begins charging Squidward and SpongeBob for the right to even work at the Krusty Krab.

According to the German philosopher and political economist Karl Marx (1818–1883), Krabs is guilty of commodifying his fellow sea creature, meaning that he views them as important only insofar as they can commercially serve his interests.[2] His employees are useful merely because they are necessary to operate the Krusty Krab, and his patrons are valuable only when spending money. Thus, when Krabs sees customers leaving his restaurant, he wails, "That's me money walkin' out the door," demonstrating that his concern for them lies only in financial

---

[2] Karl Marx, *Das Kapital* (Regnery, 2000).

transaction. Similarly, Krabs not only dehumanizes (or "de-sea-creature-izes") his customers into implements of economic exchange, he attempts to turn his employees into mere commodities.

At its most extreme form, the commodification of labor is slavery, where individuals are quite literally bought and sold and traded. Krabs is not above such despicable acts. In "Welcome to the Chum Bucket," Krabs wagers— and loses—SpongeBob in a game of poker against Plankton. He then treats his fry cook as if he owned him by forcing him to go to work for the Chum Bucket. Less blatant and more common, however, are the efforts to buy and sell the labor of individuals in a market place, which leads to their being viewed in commercial terms. Krabs is certainly guilty of this form of commodification of his employees, as Squidward and SpongeBob are consistently devalued and debased, transformed into objects with a price tag, just like a $24.95 blender, a $32.50 toaster, or a $62.67 juicer ("Krab Borg").

The commodification of his employees leads Krabs not only to view them as objects rather than as individuals with a right to claim basic dignity and fair treatment, it also leads him to engage in unjust practices. In "Can You Spare a Dime?" Krabs places the value of a single dime above that of his long-time employee, Squidward, whom he fires after accusing him of taking the coin (even though it was in Mr. Krabs's pocket the whole time).

Krabs is enriched not by his own efforts, but by exploiting SpongeBob's gentle naivety and using the fry cook's labor to profit himself. Ultimately, SpongeBob's work is going not only to support himself in the form of his wages, he is also working to directly enrich Krabs, who is never shown doing any more work than counting his money. This relationship is something that Marx referred to as the "rate of exploitation" (the ratio of the time a worker spends laboring to earn her own paycheck versus the amount of time she spends working towards generating the profit of her employer). In "The Original Fry Cook" we learn that SpongeBob's predecessor, Jim, quit the Krusty Krab when Krabs refused to give him a raise.

Although the stated and implied amount of money being paid to SpongeBob and Squidward varies from episode-to-episode, it is reasonable to assume that they get paid no more than (and perhaps even illegally below) minimum wage ("Dying for Pie"). On the other hand, Krabs, who is not the one laboring in the hot kitchen, has earned over a million dollars from the Krusty Krab in his lifetime ("Clams"). Krabs is obviously unconcerned about Marxist notions of exploitation. Should anyone (namely Squidward) make the charge that Krabs is being unfair, Mr. Krabs directs them to *The Krusty Krab Employee Manual*, second revised edition; page 35; section 19; Clause 3B: "The proprietor reserves the right to be unfair" ("Can You Spare a Dime?").

How Can I Be Okay when Me Money's Gone?

Given what we know about Krabs, what stops us from labeling him the quintessential villain of the series? What is it that keeps us applauding his ability to thwart Plankton while still finding his particular pursuit of profit so profoundly perverse? The answer lies in his inversion of the proper moral order, taking things that are valued as means to an end and making them ends in themselves. To clarify this, we have to distinguish between intrinsic and instrumental forms of value.

Intrinsic goods are those things that require no external or additional justification; they are good for their own sake. A common philosophical example of an intrinsic good is happiness. Happiness is a state of being that is an end-in-itself. We don't desire happiness because it helps us achieve other higher goals. Happiness *is* the goal we seek, and many other qualities or goods are valued only insofar as they help us to obtain this end. These other, instrumental goods (often referred to in philosophical circles as extrinsic goods) can be thought of as tools whose value is found in their ability to help us achieve some other end. Just as a spatula is a tool that is used to flip a Krabby Patty in order to create the delectable sandwich treat loved the ocean-over, instrumental or extrinsic goods are held to be important because they help us to create or achieve our desired end.

Adam Smith (1723–1790), is the founder of modern capitalist economics. Smith argued that money and markets served to allow people to pursue their own interests, not that they were ends in themselves. Smith, who largely influenced thinkers like Rand, saw the value of money as resulting from other valued factors (in particular, a person's labor) and instrumental in satisfying other ends. As a moral philosopher, Smith was concerned with the organization of markets not to principally serve economic growth, but to facilitate greater levels of human happiness. In fact, he is concerned primarily with "the happiness and perfections of man . . . not only as an individual, but as a member of a family, of a state, and of a great society of mankind."[3] Money-making, therefore, is to serve other ends, not an end in itself.

The Greek philosopher Aristotle (384–322 B.C.E.)— who devoted a substantial amount of his work to defining what is necessary to achieve a state of *eudaimonia* (a life of flourishing, well-being, and happiness)—argued: "The life

---

[3] Adam Smith, *An Inquiry into the Nature and Causes of the Wealth of Nations* (Random House, 1937), p. 726.

of money-making is undertaken under compulsion, and wealth is evidently not the good we are seeking; for it is merely useful for the sake of something else."[4] Aristotle ultimately viewed the pursuit of wealth as valuable only in its ability to serve meeting other needs—not the other way around. In fact, Aristotle's perspective would serve to remind Krabs that "even rich men . . . are thought to need friends most of all; for what is the use of such prosperity without the opportunity of benefice, which is exercised chiefly and in its most laudable form towards friends?"[5]

In *SpongeBob SquarePants*, as in our own lives, money is to be viewed as an instrumental good. When the Flying Dutchman gives Krabs the "gift" of being able to hear his money talk, it demands that the miser spend it on a variety of other goods. The money is actually asking Krabs to view it properly, as a means to satisfy his wants and needs, and not as something to be valued for its own sake. Rather than spending it on these other things, however, Krabs wants to hoard the money, choosing at one point to bury it rather than spend it.

Whereas Rand suggests that money is both a tool of exchange to help people seek their wants in an open market and an indicator of other valuable traits like creativity, intellect, physical prowess, the development of essential skills, or a willingness to work hard, even she would argue that it ought not be viewed as a good in and of itself. Yet Krabs often places money even ahead of his own well-being. In "Clams," when a giant, blue-lipped clam eats Krabs's millionth dollar, Krabs keeps SpongeBob and Squidward hostage on his boat—the S.S. Cheapskate—dumping all their food except for a single

---

[4] *Nichomachean Ethics* (Oxford University Press, 1998), Book I, Chapter 5, lines 1096a5–7.

[5] *Nichomachean Ethics*, Book VIII, Chapter 1, lines 1155a1–2.

sandwich overboard. After tying his crew up and using them as live bait to attract the clam, Krabs sacrifices himself to "Ol' Blue-Lips" by jumping into its mouth to retrieve the bill. The clam closes its mouth while Krabs celebrates. SpongeBob and Squidward think their employer has been taken to his doom when Krabs resurfaces with his dollar. He made a trade with the giant clam, his one millionth dollar in exchange for Krabs's body—something Krabs said was "nothing important."

Examples of Krabs transvaluing money, re-evaluating it as an intrinsically good end rather than as a tool to instrumentally achieve other, higher values, are present throughout the series. In "One Krab's Trash," he once more risks his safety by taking on a graveyard full of the undead to try and get back a novelty hat he thinks is worth one million dollars, while in "Arrgh!" he becomes so obsessed by the thought of treasure after playing a board game with Patrick and SpongeBob that he leads them on a seemingly insane quest for the fictional treasure.

As chance would have it, they accidentally discover a treasure belonging to the Flying Dutchman, a ghost that haunts the waters under the sea. However, the Dutchman takes the treasure back for himself, giving SpongeBob and Patrick each their own gold doubloon, while Krabs is given a piece of plastic that looks like the actual treasure chest containing the Dutchman's booty. Perhaps most notably, in "Money Talks," we find that Krabs has sold his soul several times over in order to make a quick buck.

Krabs has created a fetish out of money, something that, when properly viewed, has instrumental and not intrinsic value. What Krabs has done is to invert the proper understanding of the good, converting the means to ends and vice-versa. Rather than viewing money as an instrument to help him seek other goods on his quest for fulfillment, flourishing and happiness, he often sacrifices those things in pursuit of more and more wealth.

Moreover, Krabs places the value of money above the well-being of others, which is not surprising for someone who names his cash register "Cashie" and says that it's "the closest thing to a friend he has ever had" ("SpongeBob SquarePants vs. The Big One"). In "Whale of a Birthday," Krabs allows his cheapness to ruin Pearl's—his only child's—sixteenth birthday by trying to cut corners at every possible turn. He replaces the requested ice-sculpture of Pearl with a statue made of expired Krabby Patty meat, and hires Squidward to stand-in for the entire pop-band, "Boys Who Cry."

SpongeBob had been following Pearl around with Mr. Krabs's credit card and purchased for her everything she actually wanted. While we may debate the ethical considerations of trying to buy someone's temporary pleasure, Pearl, who thought Krabs was actually getting her the things she wanted, was made to feel that she was more important to her father than money. We, the viewing audience, know differently, however. When he starts up the short-lived *Krusty Kronicle* newspaper, Krabs pushes SpongeBob into writing sensationalized stories (sometimes using "editorial privilege" to embellish the stories even further) that damage the reputation of Mrs. Puff, Larry the Lobster, Plankton, and Sandy Cheeks ("The Krusty Kronicle"). In "Born Again Krabs" he sells SpongeBob's soul to the Flying Dutchman for a mere sixty-two cents.

Know Thyself, Krabs

I don't claim that Krabs has perverse values because he is an entrepreneurial success, but in spite of that. The problem is that Krabs never seems to learn from the suffering he undergoes, or from witnessing the pain and struggles he inflicts on others. He doesn't seem to be an inherently bad person who enjoys making others suffer, nor a sadist who enjoys suffering himself. Instead, Krabs seems to lack a true knowledge of himself and what would make him truly happy. In fact, without money Krabs seems incredibly uncomfortable with himself and his life, as witnessed in his short-lived retirement ("Selling Out"), his lack of friendships ("Mid-Life Crustacean"), and his inability to relate to his daughter in much more than commercial terms ("Whale of a Birthday"). He has never taken the time to evaluate what is truly important, nor can we say he is an individual who is leading a life of real meaning. In a manner of speaking, Krabs is less a nefarious miser and more a tragically unfulfilled figure who is blind to the means of achieving his own happiness.

Perhaps it is in this that we, like SpongeBob, see something vulnerable and likable in Krabs. Quite often, it seems, it is easy to allow our own lives to take on the inversion of values represented in Mr. Krabs.[6] People fall victim to drug abuse and alcoholism, give into gluttony that leads to problems of obesity or extreme debt, and otherwise seek a variety of hollow pursuits that show a perversion of a virtuous order that might produce real happiness. In terms of wealth and commodities, we need a source of income in order to provide for our basic needs, which money instrumentally helps us fulfill, but beyond the

---

[6] In 2008, the average American with children, between the ages of twenty-five and fifty-four, spent more time working, nearly nine hours each day, than any other activity. Compare that to the less than three hours each day Americans spend on "leisure and sports." In fact, work, sleep, eating, and doing household chores, accounted for over eighteen hours in a twenty-four hour period (roughly seventy-seven percent). Bureau of Labor and Statistics, "Charts from the American Time Use Survey," *American Time Use Survey* (February 23rd, 2010), <www.bls.gov/tus/charts/>.

meeting of those needs we might begin to ask ourselves whether we're truly happier by seeking higher levels of wealth by working longer hours, rather than spending time with family or friends, or enjoying leisurely time, or pursuing a life of emotional, spiritual, or philosophical development. Wealth is valuable because it affords a life we wish to live. But without a true understanding of ourselves and what is important for achieving a state of well-being and happiness, there is a danger that we will chase more and more material wealth and consumer goods to the point of actually taking us farther from the happiness we seek.[7]

So, You Tried to Kill Me Over a Little New Age Management, Eh?

Human beings seek a life of happiness, but unfortunately, like Krabs, many of us tend to confuse the means—money, status, possessions—with the ends. Not even Rand would support Krabs in this regard. As her character d'Anconia says, "Money will not purchase happiness for the man who has no concept of what he wants: money will not give him a code of values, if he's evaded the knowledge of what to value, and it will not provide him with a purpose, if he's evaded the choice of what to seek" (*Atlas Shrugged*, p. 382).

---

[7] Empirical studies on the impact of the pursuit of wealth beyond the fulfillment of basic needs on happiness and well-being have found that wealth has a diminishing marginal return after taking a person a bit beyond a subsistence life-style. Moreover, those studies have also shown a marked tendency for the wealthiest countries of the world to report decreased levels of happiness with greater levels of economic growth. In such cases, wealth is shown to have an empirically instrumental effect in terms of helping us meet our needs and provide for some level of leisure and comfort, but further pursuit of wealth beyond such basic levels reduces happiness. See Robert E. Lane, *The Loss of Happiness in Market Democracies* (Yale University Press, 2001).

Such a mistaken inversion of well-being actually drives us further and further from the life of happiness for which we are searching. Ultimately, the truly worthwhile pursuits are those virtuous activities that lead to happiness and are found in the connections we have with family, friends, community, and the development of the self. With such possibilities for happiness in mind, we hope that Krabs, and all of us, will one day learn the true value of a dollar.[8]

[8] A special thanks to my colleague and friend Timothy Dunn with whom I first explored the transvaluation of extrinsic goods to intrinsic ones by creating a fetish out of those things that otherwise hold only instrumental value in a chapter in Dean A. Kowalski, ed., *The Philosophy of the X-Files* (University Press of Kentucky, 2007), pp. 142–158.

5
I'm Just a Squirrel

DENISE DU VERNAY

In a 2000 episode of *SpongeBob SquarePants* titled "Squirrel Jokes," SpongeBob, while performing stand-up comedy, is bombing terrifically. We, the viewers, feel for him and want him to succeed, but not in the way he chooses. Suddenly, he gets the brilliant idea to tell squirrel jokes (equivalent to the demeaning "blonde joke") with Sandy Cheeks, Bikini Bottom's only resident rodent, as the butt.

Sandy is offended and angry with SpongeBob until he tells her that he was joking and that everyone knows she's the "smartest one in town." This placates her. If the episode had ended here, it would be okay to pass the episode off as anti-feminist or mindless. Instead, the episode continues. Sandy discovers that others in town are taking the jokes seriously, including a mother who snatches her child away from Sandy, saying, "Don't stand so close to the squirrel, Billy. You'll catch its stupid." Sandy remarks, "stupidity isn't a virus, but it sure is spreading like one."

Sandy has had enough, so she teaches SpongeBob a lesson by behaving in the stupid manner his jokes indicate, scaring him pantsless in the process and causing him to change his comedy from being squirrel-specific to picking on the foibles of all of Bikini Bottom's residents, including himself. SpongeBob and the viewer have learned valuable lessons: do not underestimate the damaging effects of negative stereotypes and do not underestimate the power of Sandy Cheeks.

Although Sandy is featured infrequently, her presence is proof—perhaps the only proof—that the show promotes feminist messages. Indeed, Sandy is enough to make the overall tone of the show pro-female, even though the show frequently relies on stereotypes and its cast is largely made up of male characters.

While the show doesn't give all that much focus to its female characters, this fact certainly doesn't get in the way of a feminist discussion within the show. The character of Sandy Cheeks (who we know is the smartest one—not "smartest woman" or "smartest squirrel" but smartest one—in Bikini Bottom) offers opportunities to discuss femininity and different types of feminism illustrated on SpongeBob SquarePants, and in fact, the male characters also offer an interesting window through which to view feminism. The fact that *SpongeBob SquarePants* is a Nickelodeon show should also not be overlooked; Nickelodeon has promoted "girl power" culture.[1]

Feminism Beyond the Treedome

Firstly, the word "feminism" means a lot of things to a lot of people, and I will clarify and define some types of feminism as they're commonly used. "Sex" refers to biological distinctions and "gender" refers to social constructs of femininity or masculinity. Although "girl power" as a slogan encouraging the empowerment of girls (specifically, the contexts of Nickelodeon's 1990s initiative, the Spice Girls, and "Girls Rule" T-shirts) was more or less an ele-

---

[1] Sarah Banet-Weiser, *Kids Rule! Nickelodeon and Consumer Citizenship* (Duke University Press, 2007), p. 105.

ment of "commodity feminism," an attempt to sell a particular image of strength to young girls, the long-term effects of the ideology seem positive overall. At the very least, the initiative put the spotlight on Nickelodeon shows with female leads (*Clarissa Explains It All*, *Dora the Explorer*, *As Told by Ginger*) and eventually brought the character Sandy Cheeks to television.

Probably because it was created and developed entirely by men, *SpongeBob SquarePants* is male-centric. In addition to having few female characters, all of whom play only supporting roles, they tend to be unpleasant, excluding, of course, Sandy Cheeks. However, because SpongeBob is a sea sponge, he is asexual, which raises a question regarding how much of his behavior can be attributed to maleness or to masculinity. So while SpongeBob and Patrick are male, are they actually "men," with all the positive and negative connotations that accompany that word? I think most viewers would agree that the answer is no.

A materialist feminist view of *SpongeBob SquarePants* would more likely feel for SpongeBob's plight over any of the female characters' situations. Because materialist feminism is more concerned with material social inequality than biological sex, the issue of SpongeBob's oppression is the biggest cause for concern on the show. While it's true that gender inequality is part of what materialist feminists analyze, Mr. Krabs's abuse of his employees, especially SpongeBob, would probably be the most troubling to the materialist feminist. Especially upsetting is the way that Mr. Krabs exploits SpongeBob's good nature and strong work ethic. SpongeBob as worker and even property is perhaps best exemplified in the episode "Welcome to the Chum Bucket" in which Mr. Krabs loses SpongeBob to Plankton in a poker game and actually hands him over. The hierarchy illustrated through Plankton and Mr. Krabs is comparable to an old boys' club. The duo demonstrates the ways that abuses of capitalism lead to oppression of the lower classes.

Sandy Cheeks, on the other hand, is what is known as a liberal feminist. A liberal feminist is one who seeks to attain equality with men, not by trying to change the system, but by working within the status quo. In this case, Sandy is a female who has attained equality with males by being a maverick—it's no coincidence that Sandy is a Texan. Although she's generally kind and fun, she will become agitated if her friends are in danger or if her beloved Texas is insulted. Being strong-willed works not only with the outspoken Texan stereotype, it also works to accent Sandy's characterization as a tough woman functioning in the old boys' club. Sandy's role as scientist, inventor, iconoclast, and "smartest one" in Bikini Bottom certainly depicts a female character as able to not only play with the boys, but in this case, beat the boys.

Stereotypes in SpongeBob SquarePants

Several stereotypes depicted on SpongeBob SquarePants appear to prevent positive work in promoting a materialist feminist agenda, but their presence can facilitate a useful discussion of stereotypes and potential reasons why children's shows rely on them so frequently. Consider Mr. Krabs, the stingy and greedy business owner. Although he is not evil to the level of *The Simpsons*' Monty Burns (that is more Plankton's cup of chum), he is cheap and stubborn. Whether he's refusing to toss a rotted Krabby Patty or he's making SpongeBob work overtime without time-and-a-half, Mr. Krabs will do what it takes to maintain the status quo and save a buck.

Mr. Krabs has a difficult daughter (who, curiously, is a whale). While some of her frustration is justified (considering the closest to pizza her father is willing to provide for her slumber party is a snack of crackers with ketchup), a tantrum that involves locking her father out of the house is not acceptable behavior. The teenage-daughter-as-spoiled-brat motif is just as tired and predictable in American television as the stupid best friend motif (yes, I'm talking about you, Patrick) or the unpleasant boss.

Plankton's wife, Karen, is a computer of his own creation, but yet even she is a stereotype of an unsupportive, know-it-all, nagging wife. Why would he create a shrew for himself? Probably for the same reason that so many other characters on this show and in many, many other childrens' shows are stereotypes: It is simply easier to rely on existing tropes. Moreover, the motif of the nagging wife is certainly an issue worthy of dissection in dealing with a young audience, along with the spoiled teen daughter and the stupid best friend.

However, there is a pearl in the oyster: the character of Sandy Cheeks. Although she is not featured frequently, Sandy is a redeeming feature of the show and offsets, to a large degree, the negativity surrounding the other female characters. Sandy is a refreshing iconoclast. She's a gutsy scientist from Texas. When another character on the show needs to be schooled, Sandy does it. She is a terrestrial mammal who lives under the sea in a special suit of her own design. She uses her smarts to keep herself alive in an environment she's not built for. By breaking the rules—while still respecting them—she's a positive role model for the children who watch the show. Even with her well-documented smarts, she is not immune to misjudgments, such as the "Squirrel Jokes" example above. The success of SpongeBob's jokes opens the doors to discuss other stereotypes (dumb blondes, hot-tempered redheads, racial stereotypes) so children can begin to understand where stereotypes come from and why they can't be relied upon.

Sandy and Femininity

As the only terrestrial character, Sandy Cheeks lives in her own treedome and wears a suit and dome on her head. The not-so-subtle girly symbol (the flower on her dome) shows there is no reason why science and ingenuity cannot be in harmony with femininity. In fact, in the 2009 episode "Overbooked," Sandy tells SpongeBob (while wearing a bikini, no less), "I whipped up a new invention that I'm going to unveil tonight in front of my comrades." Later, while she's giving her presentation (a cloning machine), she's wearing an adorable halter dress. Her appearance is feminine but does not interfere with how seriously her audience, who seem to be largely male, treats her.

About a year ago, a thirteen-year-old boy (who watches the show with his two very young little sisters) remarked to me, "Sandy's smart, a bodybuilder, and an independent squirrel." I was immediately glad that Sandy Cheeks existed, until he continued, "I think she's a lesbian." Clearly, he must not have noticed the flower on her dome. Being called a lesbian isn't an insult, per se, but the assertion that for a female character to be smart, athletic, and independent automatically means she must be a lesbian is, indeed, insulting. His identification of Sandy Cheeks as gay probably does not come from her personality or behavior on the show but probably was either picked up from something an adult said or, if I'm giving him quite a bit of credit, a misanalysis of what he thought the creators were trying to achieve through Sandy Cheeks. Even though it seems an isolated judgment of Sandy, I find this stereotype disheartening in general—that to be a strong, independent iconoclast, she must be a lesbian.

Of course, there are lots of assumptions made about Sandy's heterosexuality, or, more likely, asexuality, than potential homosexuality. For instance, Sandy has been romantically linked to Larry the Lobster, and it is often suggested that SpongeBob may also have a crush on Sandy. Many fans on SpongeBob discussion boards and blogs refer to Sandy as SpongeBob's girlfriend, and the only comments made by adult fans of the show that discuss the possibility that Sandy is a lesbian are purely facetious and done in response to the Great Gay SpongeBob Controversy of 2005. This is what I'm calling the debacle in 2005 when several Christian groups, most notably James Dobson's Focus on the Family, attacked the character of SpongeBob SquarePants for promoting a gay agenda.[2] But because Sandy does not date, I am compelled to believe that Sandy's sexuality is a non-issue and her function on the show is to be a literary foil to SpongeBob's other best friend, Patrick. Not only is Patrick markedly stupid, but he is generally ponderous and uninspired.

So Where Do Gay Cartoon Characters Come From?

When (often conservative) individuals and organizations sexualize a cartoon sea sponge, a purple dinosaur, a Teletubby, or even classic characters like Velma and Peppermint Patty, they are showering exactly the attention onto sexuality that they purport to reject. Furthermore, attributing sexuality to kids' TV characters only sexualizes their young fans. When I was a child, it did not occur to me or any of my friends (that I know of) that

---

[2] <www.christianitytoday.com/ct/2005/januaryweb-only/34.0c.html> and <www.nytimes.com/2005/01/20/politics/20sponge.html>.

Peppermint Patty was anything beyond a tomboy, and I'm sure the children who watch *SpongeBob SquarePants* are not looking for clues regarding SpongeBob or Sandy's sexual orientations.

It isn't until a character's sexuality is addressed by Focus on the Family and others like them that the innocence of the viewer is challenged and her worldview is altered and matured, which seems counter-intuitive to the ideals of wholesomeness these conservative organizations claim to be about. Also, by shining focus on the female body, they employ a misogynistic tactic that has historically been a means for holding back women. Considering everything from hysteria in Victorian England to PMS comments dished out in homeroom, the biological body has been a longtime enemy of women: it's something that prevents them from playing ball with the boys, or it's something to resent, to gain control over, to discipline, and, sometimes, even to starve.

By making such inflammatory claims, these groups are introducing topics of sexuality and biology to children long before it matters and potentially causing problems much earlier than necessary. This is not to say that the characterization of Sandy Cheeks is inculpable—her character is very aware of her body and even has to give in to its demands at times (she requires a special dome to breathe, for example, and she hibernates). She is a bodybuilder and mammal living in an environment hostile to her ilk. Feminist biologist Lynda Birke offers several contemporary ways women have chosen to show discipline over their bodies, among them body piercing, bodybuilding, and cosmetic surgery.[3] In the process of showing her empowerment, Sandy is also showing her domination over

---

[3] Lynda Birke, *Feminism and the Biological Body* (Rutgers University Press, 2000), p. 33.

her body. (One could argue that, in addition to body-building, her special suit is a form of body modification.) But this kind of analysis, done by scholars and critics, is not the kind of analysis done by children: to children, Sandy is a squirrel, scientist, and SpongeBob's friend. For those child viewers, she is a much-needed example of a smart, female character.

The diversity of the male and female characters in *SpongeBob SquarePants*, although living under the sea, is almost reflective of the diversity of any playground. Of course, sexualizing asexual characters undermines the perceived safety of the show to those gullible enough to believe the attacks: the parents who forbid their children from watching the show to the children who then wonder why.

After All, Who's the Toughest Critter in Bikini Bottom?

I suspect that the show survived the assaults unscathed and might even benefit from these baseless attacks. Since its start in 1999, the show has maintained its popularity with children, has grown even more popular with adults, and has always had an abundance of celebrity guest stars. Support for SpongeBob goes beyond the show directly; for example, "Weird Al" Yankovic consistently includes a SpongeBob T-shirt as one of his many costume changes in his live shows. Since 2005 (when Focus on the Family began assailing *SpongeBob*), an interesting selection of guests have appeared on the show, including Victoria Beckham, Ernest Borgnine, David Bowie, Tim Conway, Johnny Depp, Ian McShane, Patton Oswalt, and Dennis Quaid.

Sandy Cheeks is infrequently featured, but when she's around, she's the brains and the voice of reason on the show, whether she's reassuring SpongeBob that there are no such things as aliens or trying to get her pesky friends SpongeBob and Patrick out of the way of her work on an important project. The episode "Sandy's Rocket" is an example of both. Sandy has a terrific line in this one: "This is science: I don't have time for fun and games and I don't have time for stowaways."

Sandy is the grown-up. She's a proud Texan living far from home, she's a squirrel who lives under the sea, and she's a body-building karate buff who wears a flower on her dome. These attributes are not offered as contradictions, but rather as interesting complexities in a female cartoon character. Sandy Cheeks is one strong reason why *SpongeBob SquarePants* is good for kids and, yes, good for feminism.

6

He Went to College (And Other Reasons We Should Serve Plankton)

Nicolas Michaud

With the cry, "I went to college!" Sheldon J. Plankton asserts his superiority over the rest of the inhabitants of Bikini Bottom. For many, Plankton is an inept villain with an overly inflated concept of his own intellect. When observing his actions and interactions, we're generally expected to sympathize with SpongeBob and Mr. Krabs who regularly must thwart Plankton's plans.

In the short term, Plankton seeks the secret of the Krabby Patty, but his long-term goal is world domination. We breathe easily knowing that Plankton will not succeed, largely due to the efforts of our so-called heroes' interventions. But, we may be taking this breath too soon. This common way of looking at Plankton and SpongeBob is misguided, and the inhabitants of Bikini Bottom unfairly repress Plankton.

If we examine Plankton's actions by using some of the perspectives of philosopher Friedrich Nietzsche (1844–1900), we realize that his attempt to overcome actually make him a kind of "super-human" (or, in this case, a "super-organism"). Ultimately, Plankton may actually be the unsung hero of the series, and SpongeBob the true villain.

Our Hero . . . Plankton!

To understand how impressive this much-maligned proto-zoan actually is, let's take a closer look at Plankton. Plankton is, by many counts, the most intelligent inhabitant of Bikini Bottom, perhaps even of the entire ocean. Ironically, some fans may take perverse pleasure from watching Plankton fail because of this superior intellect, which may make him unrelatable. His failures, however, do not change the fact that Plankton is a brilliant inventor. Over and over, we see him produce masterful and magnificent inventions, whether it's a robotic Mr. Krabs or a chemical composition analyzer.

Okay, so Plankton's a genius. But beyond that, he possesses many other impressive qualities. Plankton is driven, ambitious, and industrious. He regularly generates plans of action, and unlike many of us who have great ideas but fail to act on them, Plankton really, really, REALLY tries to make them happen. While most of us are busy watching the adventures of Mermaid Man and Barnacle Boy on the boob tube, Plankton is inventing, developing, and building. He spends very little time, pining over his failures and, with great tenacity, gets back on the sea horse and tries again. For Plankton, failure is not an option.

What's equally impressive about Plankton is his ability to command respect despite his stature and background. Plankton is tiny. Do you realize how hard it is to get respect when everyone is looking down at you? Imagine coming into the world trying to be a successful businessorganism, having your partner and best friend—Krabs—betray you ("Friend or Foe"), and having to overcome the fact that everyone around you feels like they are better than you are because they are tall.

Likewise, consider Plankton's background. His entire family is comprised, frankly, of idiots. Thousands of morons! ("Plankton's Army") Given what we've seen in terms of his interactions with his family, it isn't likely that he was provided the nurturing support and attention he might have deserved given his unusual intelligence. Still, Plankton went to college. He struggled to make something of himself beyond the simple pursuit of his relatively simple (what else can we call a single-celled organism?) family. Plankton has had to overcome the kind of odds that most of us would find crippling: small stature, unsupportive family life, betrayal by closely trusted comrades. And, in many respects, he has succeeded. We shouldn't mock Plankton. We should be impressed!

Super-Plankton!

Now that we know something about the true hero of our story, we can consider why it is that everyone else in Bikini Bottom tries to hold him back. If we review some of the work of one of philosophy's most influential thinkers, Friedrich Nietzsche, we can understand why others feel such a deep need to prevent Plankton's success. Nietzsche was a German philosopher who argued that our way of looking at morality is deeply mistaken. Nietzsche writes, famously, about a super-man who is superior to the common person. Such an individual would find hostility and imposed restraint because of the common person's resentment that individuals to hold this super-man back.

You might say that applying Nietzsche to Plankton is misguided because Plankton doesn't exhibit all of the superior qualities of the Nietzschian super-man; namely a lack of resentment toward the common person. The super-man, unlike the common person, does not feel antipathy toward others, and instead will harbor deep feelings of good will towards the lesser individuals. However, it may be that the oppressive forces of Bikini Bottom have for so long abused and berated the little copepod that he uses his hostility as a defense mechanism in a manner Nietzsche might not have anticipated from his super-man. Plankton is capable of friendship and care for others (for example in "Best Frenemies," "F.U.N.," and "New Leaf"), but the actions of others always attack him, until he has no recourse but to retreat back into his own hostile acts.

The Nietzschian super-man is better than others are because he chooses to be better, and because he is stronger physically or mentally. The key point is that he knows what he wants and he seeks the fulfillment of those wants. Nietzsche argues that his super-man has what he terms the "will-to-power." The super-man does not let anything get in his way, and those who are lesser find themselves having to do his will. Some, like Plankton, are just better than the rest. As Nietzsche tells us in his book *Thus Spake Zarathustra*, "men are not equal: thus speaks Justice," dismissing the popular belief that "all men are created equal." Humans are not all created equal, says Nietzsche, since some men are simply stronger, faster, or smarter. Beyond this, what really puts the "super" in super-man for Nietzsche is the superior will to power—ambition which drives us to achieve more and struggle to reach the highest position we can in life—that Plankton clearly demonstrates.

The will to power is an idea that has its beginning in the German pessimist philosopher Arthur Schopenhauer's (1788–1860) notion of the "will to live." The will to live is the idea that everything that is alive strives to live. Everything seeks to continue its own life. In ways that are similar to the will to live, according to Nietzsche, every living thing has the will to power. The will to power though is even stronger than the will to live. We prove this fact every time we risk our lives for power. The will to power is not just the desire to dominate others. It's the desire to overcome. Specifically, it is the desire to overcome oneself.

It is this "self-overcoming" that best describes the will to power. By this, I just mean that a super-man like Plankton, seeks to grow beyond himself. Super-organisms overcome their weakness and thus become stronger. Like Plankton, they overcome the mocking of others, family, and even the betrayals of their friends in order to perfect who they are. The fact that this causes the super-man to ultimately become better than other men, and then achieve dominion over them, is just a side effect. Surely, we can't blame Plankton for desiring to rule the world. After all, it is only because he is better than everyone else.

According to Nietzsche, it is good to be the super-man. The Nietzschean super-man is not the wimp that we might think of when we think of a good person, like say the rather simple-minded SpongeBob. The super-man does not show things like compassion and pity. No, he exhibits the qualities that best lead one to success in the will to power. In seeking this kind of perfection, traits like courage, open-mindedness, and truthfulness best bring one to power. He is often even willing to help others to achieve self-perfection. Think about how Plankton tried to help SpongeBob be more assertive ("Walking Small"). But SpongeBob wouldn't listen, despite Plankton so generously demonstrating how one should go about achieving greatness. Mr. SquarePants continued being all wimpy and nice . . . ew!

Nietzsche did not think that this super-man existed during his own time, nor did he believe that he himself was the super-man. He thought that this super man was a man of the future, one who was to come. This man would travel up the long and arduous road of knowledge and self-reflection. After doing this, and overcoming many trials—much like Plankton overcoming his familial background I might add—this super-man would realize the real nature of the world; that morality as we normally think of it is not true. Granted, according to Nietzsche this man would then also climb down the mountain in order to share his love and great insight with others. Because once you realize the true nature of the world and reality, you are filled with so much overwhelming love that you can't help but want to show others the real nature of the world so that they can also be free. Perhaps one day Plankton will realize such a possibility.

Why Lesser Fish Hate Plankton

Nietzsche asserts that morality is not a truth but a matter of subjective interpretation. In fact the real truth of the universe is rather random, chaotic, and comically tragic. People create morality and rules out of this chaos to hold back the super-man in order to prevent him from asserting his superiority over themselves. We tell people better than us to be compassionate and to show mercy, but the super-man should not be compassionate—at least not in the way we normally think of it. This might seem cold, but compassion, much like pity, actually demeans the person for whom you have it. It makes them lesser, you feel sorry for them. Even worse, for Plankton, compassion could get in his way.

It's not that Nietzsche believed that we should all go around hurting each other, far from it. However, we ought to be wary of how emotions like compassion are used to keep power in check. Nietzsche believed that weak people use compassion and pity as a way to keep the powerful from achieving their ends. The weak don't want to have to admit someone else is better. Even worse, they're afraid of the super-man. His will is one that naturally bends the wills of others to conform to his own. They seek pity from him, so that he will hold himself back, so that he will feel bad about being better than they are.

It is because of this manufacturing of morals designed to constrain and repress the super-man that Nietzsche had very little respect for any religion or any other institution that encouraged individuals to hold themselves back. Imagine what would happen to sharks if they felt compassion for tuna fish—the sharks would starve! Instead, the shark is constantly trying to achieve its own success and, in doing so, it achieves dominion over the tuna. We don't yell at the shark and say, "Bad shark!" So why should we tell a person who gains power over us, "Bad person"? Nietzsche argues that the super-man's will to power motivates him, as we all are—his will is just that much stronger, so we resent him or fear him. To quote Nietzsche,

> That lambs dislike great birds of prey does not seem strange: only it gives no ground for reproaching these birds of prey for bearing off little lambs. And if the lambs say among themselves; "these birds of prey are evil; and whoever is least like a bird of prey, but rather its opposite, a lamb—would he not be good?" . . . the birds of prey might view it a little ironically and say: "We don't dislike them at all, these good little lambs. We even love them: nothing is more tasty than a tender lamb." (*On the Genealogy of Morals*, Vintage, 1989, p. 44)

But, do the tuna accept the fact that they are lesser than the shark and not as worthy to rule? No. Instead, they tried to prevent Plankton, the "shark," from succeeding. Of course, that wouldn't work, so they did something far worse—they made it immoral, and asserted it was a bad thing to be a shark.

According to Nietzsche, the weak have developed what he calls a slave-morality. Whereas a master-morality judges actions based on their consequences, a slave-morality judges actions based on their intentions. Such a slave-morality causes us to evaluate SpongeBob as good because he has "kindness" in his heart, no matter how many accidents he causes or people whose lives he makes miserable.

Plankton is judged as bad because, no matter how many great things he accomplishes, his intentions are deemed ignoble. Such morality exists entirely because it prevents others from reaching super-man status, both because the weak—the slaves—are jealous of the super-man and because they don't want to have to serve him. Nietzsche has no respect for these slaves. Instead of seeking their own self-overcoming, as they should, to become great themselves, they revel in their weakness and praise the meek as being noble.

When we think about those around us, it seems that Nietzsche might have at least one thing right in that individuals have a tendency to embrace mediocrity in themselves by tearing down those who may possess superior qualities. Have you ever noticed how children will make fun of a child who is smarter, or ostracize a child who is stronger, than they are? Or the way that someone who expresses themselves differently will be mocked and scorned? This happens in the adult world, too. As soon as someone rises to a position of greatness, there are always those who secretly—and sometimes openly—hope to see him fail. People actually seem to enjoy building-up a hero only to search for ways to tear her down. Such is the way SpongeBob is praised as noble for trying to hold Plankton back. You're supposed to feel bad for SpongeBob when he falls under Plankton's superior will, when, in fact, SpongeBob is just manipulating you. SpongeBob is using your feelings of pity as a way to prevent you from realizing the truth—that Plankton is better!

That Naive Cube! How Long Must I Suffer This?

Plankton often gives SpongeBob the chance to succeed, to better himself. For example, Plankton generously tutors SpongeBob in assertiveness ("Walk Small"), offers SpongeBob friendship ("Plankton!"), and gives him the chance to work for him ("Welcome to the Chum Bucket"). SpongeBob, though, doesn't seem to get it. As Plankton has said of SpongeBob, he's "completely idiotic."

This may seem a harsh criticism, but what's so admirable about a creature who believes that if he rips his pants enough, people will want to be his friend ("Ripped Pants")? And why should we praise an individual who celebrates their own ignorance with odes to "idiot friends" ("Pest of the West")? His big empty sheep eyes stare about and just suck the intelligence out of the room. And you know what . . . everyone loves him for it. When push comes to shove, the masses love SpongeBob because he's so painfully mediocre. Nietzsche holds disdain for this mediocrity, and bemoans that the most industrious of us, the most passionate for success, are looked down upon. Those who go around hurting themselves ("A Life in a Day") and others (lest we forget that SpongeBob's antics in "Bubble Buddy" caused Scooter to drown) are considered cute, and friendly, and—go figure—make excellent employees. SpongeBob is good at taking orders.

It is in evaluating the treatment of SpongeBob at work that we find the most telling example of how Plankton is unfairly judged as being the primary antagonist of the series. Plankton is actually far better to SpongeBob than Krabs is. Plankton gives SpongeBob the chance to succeed. He pushes him, treats him almost as an equal. Of course, while the mediocre SpongeBob can't be Plankton's equal, when Plankton pushes him he is actually showing

SpongeBob respect. Plankton is saying, in effect, "I will not treat you as if you are weaker than I am. I will attempt to overcome you as if you were an equal!"

Krabs, on the other hand, uses SpongeBob. Krabs's corporate and extraordinarily greedy nature subjugates SpongeBob not because Krabs is overcoming SpongeBob through the superiority of his will, but because he uses SpongeBob's ignorance to help enslave him. Krabs came upon the secret of the Krabby Pattie by accident. And, yet, he is willing to capitalize on that accident without feeling as if he should really benefit anyone else financially. He uses his employees, pays them pathetically, and demeans them every day as servants to his greedy will. Krabs gladly keeps SpongeBob ignorant of the true nature of the world. He uses SpongeBob's naivety against him. Krabs makes everyone else think that Plankton is the villain, when, in actuality, Krabs is just a greedy idea-stealer who uses his workers as slaves to squeeze pennies out of his customers.

And yet, it's still not Krabs who's the real villain. The greedy crustacean is at least trying to achieve something for himself. He is no super-organism, he is not trying to perfect himself, but he is, at least, and often in morally questionable ways, willing to seek his own well-being. It is in praising SpongeBob that the most nefarious evil is exposed. SpongeBob is the true bad guy because embracing his childish weaknesses makes us more mediocre. SpongeBob's antics encourage this mediocrity and promote a willingness to accept our own mediocre nature. He, like all other mediocre people, seeks to make the rest of us mediocre end afraid of being better. To quote Nietzsche:

These acute observers and loiterers discover that the end is approaching fast, that everything around them is corrupted and corrupts, that nothing will stand the day after tomorrow, except one type of man, the incurably mediocre. The mediocre alone have a chance of continuing their type and propagating—they are the men of the future, the only survivors: "Be like them! Become mediocre!" is now the only morality that still makes sense, that still gets a hearing. (*Beyond Good and Evil*, Oxford University Press, 1998, p. 160)

Notice that only Patrick gets to feel really good about himself around SpongeBob. Krabs wants to make too much money, Squidward, oh, heaven forbid, wants to practice his clarinet in peace, and Plankton is too hungry for power. All of them need to stop doing the things they are best at and bring them the most joy for SpongeBob to be happy. But Patrick, whose intellect could not power a one-watt light bulb, is a great friend and encouraged to continue doing as he does. Why? Because SpongeBob looks intelligent in comparison.

To Nietzsche, the willfully mediocre are the real villains, and if there is only one thing worse than being content with one's mediocrity it is the attempt to bring down those who are not. Nietzsche isn't saying that we all can be the smartest, strongest, or fastest, but we should all seek to better ourselves. To be more than what we are. What mediocre means for Nietzsche isn't so much being dumb or weak, it's being glad to be less than you could be. Patrick's problem isn't that he is unbelievably stupid; it is the fact that there's nothing about him that strives or drives to be better. People like SpongeBob and Patrick are almost the antithesis of the will-to-power. It is as if they are seeking to be more mediocre than they already are, and in doing this they make others around them more mediocre too!

So say what you want about Plankton, unlike many he us at least striving to become a better organism. While

SpongeBob laughs too loudly at his own mistakes and simplicity and Patrick drools or watches television under his rock, Plankton is trying to rule the world. Is that really such a blameworthy act? Plankton isn't going around killing other sea creatures. Yes, he is willing to push the limits of traditional morality, but why is it noble for someone to let the judgment of others hold them back?

Perhaps what really bothers fans of SpongeBob about Plankton is the fact that he is unwilling to just be happy with what he has, to just sit down and be content with the lot that life has given him. Plankton, however, will not give in! He will keep on trying to succeed, and one day he might even achieve the secret of the Krabby Patty. Then, while everyone else is busy feeling good about themselves and splitting their pants, he can delight in ruling the world.

PART II

Welcome to Bikini Bottom

7
Bikini Bottom— Best Society Ever?

SHAUN P. YOUNG

Bikini Bottom seems a pleasant enough place to live. It is a diverse community, both in terms of species—its residents notably include Sandy Cheeks, a land squirrel—and the characters and interests of its inhabitants, who seem to have a great degree of freedom to pursue life as they see fit.

Yes, competitive, belittling and, in extreme cases, deceitful and destructive behavior occurs, but it has never intentionally proven irredeemably damaging to psyche, property or life. Even when Flatts the Flounder tries to beat up SpongeBob, he is unable to do so, because SpongeBob's body merely absorbs Flatts's punches, which, consequently, cause no pain (indeed, at one point, SpongeBob suggests they tickle him). And though Scooter drowns after Bubble Buddy and SpongeBob bury him in the sand and then fail to dig him out before the onset of high tide, his death is neither deliberate nor desired.

By all appearances, Bikini Bottom does not suffer from any noteworthy social, economic or political problems. This enviable situation is achieved seemingly in the absence of any formal system of government in the traditional sense. If that's true, then the residents of Bikini Bottom have achieved what many have argued is impossible to realize without government: namely, the establishment and maintenance of a safe and stable society that provides its members with the opportunity for personal fulfillment.

The Need for Government

For thousands of years political philosophers have argued that the creation and continuation of government is critical to enabling individuals to live a "good" life. Aristotle (384–322 B.C.E.) famously claimed that humans are "political animals" who are naturally driven to establish and maintain political societies. Moreover, he concluded that the good life can be realized only within a political association—specifically, a polis (which, roughly translated, means "city-state"). Similarly, Thomas Hobbes (1588–1679) argued that a safe and decent life is possible only after individuals join together to establish a "commonwealth" that is ruled by a "sovereign" power—that is, a government. For John Locke (1632–1704), government is necessary to ensure adequate protection for one's private property, which includes one's life and liberty. Likewise, David Hume (1711–1776) maintained that individuals must live together and co-operate in order to survive, and government is needed to enforce the type of behavior that makes that co-operation possible.

Each of the above philosophers promoted a different type of government as the most effective means by which to secure the type of individual behavior that would allow for the establishment and maintenance of a desirable society.

Aristotle concluded that the ideal form of government would be rule by a single person of unequalled virtue—someone who possesses the greatest degree of courage, justness, restraint, generosity, and wisdom. However, he argued that a polity—basically, rule by the middle class—represents the best form of widely realizable government.

Hobbes, too, believed that a virtuous monarchy was the preferred form of government because it effectively eliminated the threat of faction within the government. He also suggested that an aristocracy or democracy was acceptable provided that, whichever form the government adopts, it possesses a power able to enforce security for all. And, while Hume supported a "constitutional monarchy" in which the magistrate was constrained in its rule, Locke argued in favor of a representative form of government that includes both a legislative body and an executive. Locke proposed that the people, through majority decision-making, determine the members of the legislature, which, in turn, appoints the executive (typically, a single person). The legislature establishes laws, which the executive enforces. "The people" always retain ultimate power to judge and "dismiss" either the legislature or the executive.

Across the millennia there has been vigorous and passionate debate about which model of government represents the "ideal." However, though they may disagree on specifics, political philosophers have generally agreed that some type of government is essential to living a decent life. That claim has been especially prominent among those who consider the circumstances of individuals living in societies containing a diversity of beliefs and interests. The potential for disagreement, conflict and oppression in such societies is significant, if not unavoidable. Hence, the opportunity for all residents to live a fulfilling life necessitates the presence of a permanent, institutionalized means of preventing individuals from unduly interfering in the lives of others. It's generally concluded that the mechanism best able to provide such protection is a formal government.

An Opposite Society

In many ways Bikini Bottom seems to fly in the face of all such arguments, just as in "Opposite Day" when SpongeBob purposely acted in a manner contrary to his normal behavior. While there are suggestions that the residents of Bikini Bottom are all members of a collective political association, such as in "The Smoking Peanut" when SpongeBob refers to the members of the crowd as "citizens of Bikini Bottom," we don't see much sign that a formal government in the traditional sense exists. We never witness a meeting between government officials—at least not individuals explicitly identified as such—or any discussion of public policies or laws being developed, amended or repealed. Nor is there reference to the imposing or collection of public taxes or the establishment of publicly funded programs to assist residents.

Yet, Bikini Bottom is not completely lacking the type of public agencies, services, and political figures that many would associate with the presence of a formalized system of government. For example, there is a police force, a local jail, a court, a public postal service, a Department of Health, a Department of Motor Vehicles, and a public transit system. A "mayor" officiates the start of the "Great Snail Race" and the opening of an unfinished bridge ("Doing Time"), but there is never any indication that he engages in any of the non-ceremonial activities typically associated with governance. And in "Rule of the Dumb" a representative of the "Royal Ministry" informs Patrick that he is the legitimate "king" of Bikini Bottom (though, SpongeBob seems to be the only member of Patrick's "royal court"). Similarly, King Neptune appears in a number of episodes, and though he is identified as the ruler of the entire sea and seems to possess the power necessary to have all obey his commands, there is no indication that he either regularly exercises that power over the residents of Bikini Bottom nor that he regulates their day-to-day behavior in a manner similar to that of a traditional government.

So, how is the situation in Bikini Bottom properly characterized with regard to its compatibility with the tradition of political philosophy? Look at the similarities between the features of life in Bikini Bottom and those proposed in certain models of society that deny the need for government as it is typically understood. Arguably, the most obvious candidates to examine in that group are theories of anarchism and communism.

Playing Hooky from Government

If Bikini Bottom contains no formal-institutionalized system of government, then it might be argued that it is an anarchical society. Though it is commonly associated with disorder or chaos, the word "anarchism" actually means "without a ruler." In general, anarchists believe that government is undesirable because it is an obstacle to human progress.

According to William Godwin (1756–1836), identified by many as the father of modern anarchism, institutionalized government and its supporting agencies, such as schools and religion, prevent people from living together happily. Similarly, Peter Kropotkin (1842–1921) concluded that government divides people, classes and countries. All anarchists believe that humans need freedom to progress, just as Patrick maintains that if SpongeBob wishes to experience the fun offered by the "hooks," he must disregard his promise to Mr. Krabs to avoid them. Anarchists contend that anarchism properly implemented provides complete liberty to individuals—that is, it allows people to govern themselves.

But residents of Bikini Bottom do not possess absolute individual liberty. The most obvious obstacle to such liberty is the police force, a prominent presence in Bikini Bottom, and one whose authority does not seem to be questioned. A good example of the extensive degree to which the police force constrains individual liberty is when Squidward is issued a fine for "littering" after he tosses SpongeBob's Krusty Krab employee hat onto the ground and stomps on it to demonstrate to SpongeBob the appropriate way to react to Mr. Krabs having fired the two of them for talking about striking.

Nor is the police force the only impediment to individual liberty. In "Bummer Vacation" Mr. Krabs is forced to require SpongeBob to take a vacation to avoid the Fry Cooks Union fining the Krusty Krab for unacceptable employment practices. (Once SpongeBob becomes aware that a vacation means not working, he unsuccessfully pleads to not have to take a vacation, and then spends most of his "vacation" pursuing various schemes that will enable him to return to work before his vacation is officially over.) The presence of a health inspector in Bikini Bottom also (seemingly) necessitates that Mr. Krabs and Plankton be attentive to the quality of the food they produce, or risk having their restaurants closed—a fate that befalls the Chum Bucket in the episode "Krabby Kronicle." (In fairness to Plankton, the Chum Bucket is closed not because of a customer's complaint or as a result of problems identified by the health inspector, but rather because of a claim printed in a newspaper (written by SpongeBob for Mr. Krabs), which suggests that the food produced in the Chum Bucket is made from the body parts of residents of Bikini Bottom.) And, of course, SpongeBob is constantly prevented from achieving his goal of obtaining a driver's license, something he seems unlikely to ever do—though, in "No Free

Rides" he completes "extra credit" work for Mrs. Puff and is awarded his driver's license, but never has the opportunity to use it before it is revoked.

Mr. Krabs's House of Servitude

Given the type of constraints imposed on the behavior of its residents, Bikini Bottom does not seem to qualify as an anarchical society. Perhaps Bikini Bottom has more in common with a form of sociopolitical association that, while distinct from pure anarchism, shares certain qualities with it—namely, a communist society.

The term "communism" signifies a "communal" way of life—a collective approach to obtaining, consuming and sustaining the necessities of (a good) life—an idea that has been a feature of political philosophy since the time of Plato. The most famous advocate of communism is Karl Marx (1818–1883), and I'll rely on Marx's depiction of a communist society (which he co-developed with Friedrich Engels) to assess the similarity between such a society and Bikini Bottom.

Like anarchists, Marx was concerned with the realization of human freedom. For Marx, a communist society represented the means by which to achieve that goal. In a genuinely communist society, there is no "state" (or institutionalized government) as it is traditionally understood; similarly, there is no hierarchy of socioeconomic "classes." Marx argued that the state and its supporting agencies—such as a government—are tools used by the rich (capitalist bourgeoisie) to oppress the working class and poor (the proletariat). Consequently, rather than a government, a communist society contains an administrative body that has responsibility for performing tasks essential to the effective maintenance of the society. We can easily imagine such a society providing for the establishment of agencies to help ensure public safety, such as a police force or a department of public health.

And, as seems to be the case for the residents of Bikini Bottom, the members of a communist society are free to change jobs whenever they so desire, as SpongeBob does in "Nature Pants" when he decides to quit his job at the Krusty Krab in order to go live with the jellyfish, or as Plankton does in "New Leaf" when he (seemingly) abandons the restaurant business to establish a gift shop.

However, life in Bikini Bottom also exhibits significant violations of the requirements of Marx's ideal communist society. Perhaps the most glaring of such violations is the continued presence and activities of Mr. Eugene H. Krabs.

Marx argues that in a true communist society exploitation of the working class will cease. Yet, Mr. Krabs seems regularly to exploit SpongeBob, as in "Fear of a Krabby Patty" when he decides that the Krusty Krab will remain open twenty-four hours per day, and, consequently, SpongeBob and Squidward must work twenty-four-hour shifts for forty-three days straight! And in "Spy Buddies" he threatens to fire SpongeBob unless he agrees to spy on Plankton without being paid for his efforts.

The fact that SpongeBob seems willing to accept, if not actively seek, his own exploitation does not render it acceptable according to Marx. SpongeBob might be suffering from what Marx labeled "false consciousness"—a misunderstanding of one's actual situation, perpetrated and perpetuated by the rich to oppress the poor. According to Marx, were SpongeBob able to clearly comprehend the reality of his exploitation, he would no longer accept it. There are periodic glimpses of such comprehension, as in "Clams" when SpongeBob and Squidward realize that Mr. Krabs's obsession with money could get them killed, or in *The SpongeBob SquarePants*

Movie when SpongeBob, after being denied promotion to the position of manager at the Krusty Krab 2, and suffering from a Triple Gooberry Sunrise Sundae hangover, calls Mr. Krabs a "great big jerk." However, it seems that SpongeBob's "unmasking" of his false consciousness is, at best, minimal and fleeting. His exploitation by Mr. Krabs remains a prominent feature of his life in Bikini Bottom.

Similarly, Mr. Krabs is quick to try to capitalize on any opportunity to exploit customers of the Krusty Krab. The most noteworthy example might be in "Fungus Among Us" when SpongeBob infects the customers of the Krusty Krab with a fungus that causes an unbearable itchiness. Mr. Krabs commandeers Gary in order to charge customers five dollars each to be "de-icked," despite the fact that it is only as a consequence of patronizing the Krusty Krab that they became infected.

The continuation of such behavior and the absence of any indication that there is a society-wide attempt to stop it, suggests that Bikini Bottom cannot legitimately be labeled a communist society, at least not in the Marxist sense. However, if Bikini Bottom is not anarchist nor communist, can we call it a utopia?

Squidville Realized

The word "utopia" has been translated to mean both "no place" and "good place," but it's typically understood to refer to an ideal or perfect society. A number of philosophers have developed blueprints for utopias. Plato's Republic (360 B.C.E.) is considered by many to present the framework for a utopian society. Sir Francis Bacon (1561–1626) also developed a model of a utopia, which he labeled "New Atlantis" (1624); and the most famous utopian theorist, Sir Thomas More (1478–1535), penned the novel *Utopia* (1516) to describe what he apparently saw as the perfect society—though scholars have debated whether More really believed his Utopia to be the ideal type of society. We can see that a "utopia" can assume many different forms, and may or may not contain an institution-alized government. The only feature that all utopias must share is that the people who have dreamed them up pres-ent them as ideal or perfect societies.

SpongeBob might believe Bikini Bottom to be a utopia. He has a job he enjoys immensely, a number of close friends, all of the creature comforts he seems to desire (or the ability to acquire them), and he rarely seems to be dissatisfied with his life. Patrick, too, seems to be generally quite content and happy, and the same could be said of Sandy and Mr. Krabs.

However, it also seems that such a positive outlook is not shared by all residents of Bikini Bottom. Squidward appears less than satisfied with his life. He believes his talents as an artist—a musician, a dancer, a sculptor, a painter—are woe-fully under-appreciated and, indeed, will likely always be so among the residents of Bikini Bottom. He is unenthusiastic about his job and constantly annoyed by SpongeBob and Patrick. Indeed, his efforts to secure some personal enjoy-ment are seemingly always frustrated, as in "Good Neighbors" when his attempts to pamper himself on a Sunday are completely obliterated by SpongeBob and Patrick, after they proclaim him president of the Secret Royal Order of the Good Neighbor Lodge. Even when he moves to Squidville, a gated community inhabited solely by other cephalopods (despite his name, he is an octopus) seemingly identical in all manners to him, his contented-ness is only temporary.

Plankton, too, does not seem to have a very satisfying life. To all appearances, Plankton spends all his waking hours trying to either steal the Krabby patty formula or undermine the success of the Krusty Krab by causing it to lose customers. Unfortunately, he typically fails to achieve those goals, and when he is successful, it's only temporary. Perhaps unsurprisingly, then, he regularly expresses his dissatisfaction with his life, such as in "Krabby Road" when he observes: "You know, I don't think I've had any good times."

Protecting Against the Bubble Poppin' Boys

If anarchism, communism, and utopianism all fail—at least, individually—to capture satisfactorily the situation in Bikini Bottom, are there any other theories of sociopolitical organization that might do the job? One that immediately springs to mind is the concept of a "night-watchman" state, an idea initially promoted by John Locke and, subsequently, made famous by German political philosopher Wilhelm von Humboldt (1767–1835). The idea was repackaged in the twentieth century by Robert Nozick (1938–2002) in his book *Anarchy, State and Utopia*.

According to Nozick, all individuals naturally possess certain rights, and they're entitled to use force, both to protect these rights and to extract compensation from those who violate them. He argues that people will freely join together to establish "mutual protection associations" to help safeguard their rights, especially the right to private property, just as the citizens of New Kelp City collectively proclaim SpongeBob their mayor after he restores security to the City by ridding it of the Bubble Poppin' Boys gang. In turn, others will hire private protection agencies to safeguard their rights. Eventually, the drive for economic efficiency will result in the emergence of a single dominant protection agency which, in turn, will come to possess an effective monopoly on the use of force within that society and be able to compel all residents to obey certain rules of behavior. Once such an agency has emerged, it basically operates as a government. Nozick emphasizes that the only legitimate functions of such an agency—and, indeed, government—are to protect against violence, theft, fraud, and breach of contract.

However, clearly the restrictions under which the residents of Bikini Bottom live exceed those identified as legitimate by Nozick. For example, SpongeBob is arrested for failing to invite two police officers to his party ("Party Pooper Pants"), and Sandy is arrested for public nudity after her fur is stolen by Plankton ("Someone's in the Kitchen with Sandy"). The often unpredictable and excessive legal constraints imposed upon the residents of Bikini Bottom show that Bikini Bottom isn't Nozick's idea of a night-watchman state.

An Island of Milk and Honey or Rock Bottom?

Some philosophers have argued that government could only be unnecessary in a society populated by saints who all have the resources needed to live a meaningful, fulfilling life of their own choosing, in an environment free from conflict and involuntary deprivation. Bikini Bottom is certainly not inhabited only by saints nor is it free from conflict (though, the conflict that does emerge is rarely physical). Nevertheless, it has managed to avoid the type of problems that have typically been identified as necessitating government. Moreover, it has done so using a form of collective organization that is seemingly unique among the models of sociopolitical association developed by generation upon generation of political philosophers.

Bikini Bottom is an imaginary community, so it might be argued that the failure of political philosophers to have developed a corresponding model of society should not be surprising, nor does it reflect poorly on their skills or accomplishments. However, many of the most famous models of sociopolitical association have used as counterpoints societies that in important ways are no more "real" than Bikini Bottom—think of the "states of nature" employed by philosophers such as Hobbes, Locke, and Jean-Jacques Rousseau. Accordingly, the fictitious character of Bikini Bottom neither explains the novelty of its model of governance within the history of political philosophy nor undermines its potential value as a source of useful ideas.

What can we learn from the kind of society we see in Bikini Bottom? It's not a model of perfection but neither is it a horribly oppressive society—a dystopia. Maybe that's one lesson we can take from Bikini Bottom: it's foolish to expect perfection, but there's no need to accept dystopia either. Real life, even in an imaginary underwater society, is too complex to be captured comprehensively in a single theory, a fact that Bikini Bottom appears to embody well, but one that seems to have eluded many political philosophers.[1]

---

[1] I would like to thank my good friend Phil Triadafilopoulos for initially suggesting I watch *SpongeBob*, and my daughters Amy and Faith for ensuring that I continue to do so. I would also like to thank Joseph Foy, not only for his helpful comments and suggestions, but also for pursuing this delightful project and for offering me the opportunity to be involved.

8
SpongeBob as Royal Candidate

NATHAN ZOOK

Don't be a tool for Squidward! When you see him, plaster a Vote SpongeBob poster on him! Here in Bikini Bottom, we need justice, and SpongeBob can bring it to us as Royal Krabby.

Oh, sure, some apathetic voters are too focused on stuffing their gills with Kelp Patties to get out and VOTE SPONGEBOB FOR ROYAL KRABBY! But, if they would just lay down their food for a few minutes and listen, they'd realize that SpongeBob has promised to keep stores open twenty-four hours a day. That's right! You can eat Kelp Patties at four in the morning, or four in the afternoon. You can even get Krabby Patties with extra pickles and fried sea onions at four in the morning, or four in the afternoon.

Wait a minute. I'm not really advertising Kelp Patties, Krabby Patties, or the Krusty Krab although Mr. Krabs would be delighted if I were. I'm actually advertising SpongeBob! Did I mention that SpongeBob will babysit your kids for free?

While this monologue doesn't appear in Erica Pass's book *Vote for SpongeBob* (Simon and Schuster, 2008), which humorously explores the prospects of democracy under the sea during an election Mr. Krabs cooks up between

SpongeBob and Squidward for the position of "Royal Krabby," this type of political pandering, outrageous promises, and personal attacks is what I imagine Patrick Star, SpongeBob's campaign manager, would've engaged in if given the opportunity.

Election Time in Bikini Bottom

Elections are at the core of modern political systems referred to as democracies. As a concept, democracy finds its roots in ancient Greece, where the terms *demos* (meaning "the people") and *kratos* (meaning "strength" or power") combine to refer to a political system in which the power to govern is held by the citizens of a state.

In the classical Greek system, which existed in the ancient city-state of Athens around the fifth century B.C.E., all male citizens had the right to be heard, and to discuss and vote on issues affecting the government. This was a much more direct form of democracy than what we're usually familiar with today, as modern democracies are generally representative—meaning that we don't ourselves make political decisions, but instead elect people who then act on our behalf.

In a modern democracy, there's no higher political authority than the people, and government institutions and officials are held accountable to citizens through elections. Such elections are used to measure what the majority of the people want, which is often referred to as the "will of the people," and are especially useful for allowing the majority of the people to select someone to represent their interests.

Whereas the political struggles in a democracy involve the competition of individuals and groups for the authority to make decisions, the election at the Krusty Krab had nothing to do with such lofty political goals. Mr. Krabs, the owner of the Krusty Krab, was short of cash (or at least he wasn't making as much as he would have liked). As he walked through the restaurant looking for ways to increase his cash flow, he saw a little boy munching on a Kelp Patty and wearing a crown. The boy's mother mentioned that everyone always asks the boy about the crown because "people love royalty—you know, kings, queens, princesses, all that stuff" (*Vote for SpongeBob*, p. 4).

Mr. Krabs decided to give the people of Bikini Bottom what they wanted—royalty. He declared an election for Royal Krabby to give his restaurant more pizzazz. The two candidates, Spongebob and Squidward, were hand-picked by Mr. Krabs himself to run in the election. Thanks to the campaign efforts of Patrick, SpongeBob won, and in recognition of his achievement Mr. Krabs handed him a spatula as his royal scepter and ordered him to get to work welcoming everyone into the restaurant and keeping the establishment clean. Rather than encouraging SpongeBob to fulfill his campaign promises to make Bikini Bottom a better place, Mr. Krabs names a new sandwich the "Royal Krabby Patty" after the winner and then demands that SpongeBob fit back into his position as Krusty Krab employee. SpongeBob promptly heads to the kitchen to flip Krabby Patties and forgets about the good citizens of Bikini Bottom.

What caused such a potentially admirable candidate as SpongeBob, who was actively participating in the democratic process because he felt it was his duty to the people, to forget about the voting citizens as soon as he had won the election?

One obvious explanation is that democracy in this case was little more than a sham. Mr. Krabs controlled the election and held the real power; SpongeBob and Squidward were just pawns to make it look as if he was running a democratic election. Sure, the people voted, but their preference meant little to Mr. Krabs. He had already decided the outcome of the election—it was going to be business as usual. Democracy was meaningless. Mr. Krabs set up his own election in order to secure his status and wealth in Bikini Bottom. He was giving the people a choice between two candidates that he controlled which meant there really wasn't much of a choice.

Democratic theorist C. Wright Mills (1916–1962) argued that the description of democracy as a system that tries to take into account the public opinion and aggregate will of the people is "a set of images out of a fairy tale."[1] In reality, he believed that elites establish elections to further their own interests. Much like Mr. Krabs used SpongeBob and Squidward, the power elites of contemporary political society use individuals who participate in these elections as tools to make it look as if they're following the will of the people. The losers in the democratic process are the masses of people whose will is being manipulated by the power elite.

The notion of Mr. Krabs as serving the position of "power elite" and using his influence to control others to manipulate outcomes favorable to his interests is a common theme in the *SpongeBob* franchise. Beyond the sham election of "Royal Krabby," another excellent example of SpongeBob being duped into helping prop up the elitist Mr. Krabs's interests at the expense of the majority of the population of Bikini Bottom can be seen in the book *SpongeBob Goes Green: An Earth-Friendly Adventure.*[2]

It all started with another money-making scheme by Mr. Krabs. He made a private swimming pool for the exclusive

---

[1] C. Wright Mills, *The Power Elite* (Oxford University Press, 2000), p. 298.

[2] Molly Reisner, *SpongeBob Goes Green: An Earth-Friendly Adventure* (Simon and Schuster, 2009).

use of paying customers at the Krusty Krab, and made SpongeBob pool manager. No one was coming to swim, though, because it was early spring and way too cold. Mr. Krabs got the not-so-bright idea of "pumpin' a wee bit of carbon dioxide into the air" to "warm up the temperature and bring on an endless summer!" (*SpongeBob Goes Green*, p. 10). As a loyal employee, SpongeBob quickly got to work pumping carbon dioxide. After burning tires and turning on appliances and lights all over town, the atmosphere warmed right up and people began paying to swim in the Krusty Krab Pool. Like a member of the power elite seeking his own benefit rather than the benefit of Bikini Bottom, Mr. Krabs was money-seeking.

Doom quickly came to Bikini Bottom in the form of unbearably high temperatures. The pool was filled with customers, which Mr. Krabs loved, but he complained that "this heat is frying my shell" (*SpongeBob Goes Green*, p. 15). Chaos broke out as the pool became overcrowded from the population of Bikini Bottom trying to cool off. This didn't work, though, as the water in the pool began to sizzle and then evaporate (which is especially odd and troubling for an undersea pool). SpongeBob tried to rally his friends to help, but quickly realized they had skipped town for Murky Waters. He told Mr. Krabs about global warming and they quickly made their way to Murky Waters to persuade everyone to return to Bikini Bottom.

Here, *SpongeBob* provides an important set of lessons about democracy and politics. On one hand, theorists like Mills assume that power elites control the elections in a democracy and that there's no way to challenge their domination. Such was the case in the fraudulent election for "Royal Krabby." On the other hand, education can be used to confront power elites and their claims that they have the true interests of the people at heart. This is shown through Sandy Cheeks educating SpongeBob about global warming, which he in turn used to influence Krabs. Information like this can be used, or not used, at the discretion of citizens in a democracy.

The notion of democracy assumes that citizens are competent to make rational decisions to further their own interests or the interests of the whole society.[3] It's up to the people to advance or hinder the efforts of elites like Mr. Krabs, and if they allow themselves to be manipulated it may be in part because they have allowed it. So, is democracy all it is cracked up to be?

Democracy Is Overrated

If you ask the politicians in a democracy how to run an election, they'll say the best way to do it is their way. The United States claims that it has the truest form of democracy, while Cuba claims that it has the best, and SpongeBob fans in China are probably not told that Italy does things better. In short, any modern government will be biased for its style of politics. Instead of looking to modern governments for answers on how to participate in an ideal society, let's look back at ancient Athens, the birthplace of democracy. Even if people do have the capacity to form a democracy in the face of power elites, is it even worthwhile to pursue democracy?

One of the most famous Greek philosophers, Plato (around 428–347 B.C.E.), did not favor democracy. Instead, he proposed a republic where educated Guardians ruled over the masses—a system he felt was the ideal way to form a just society. Democracy, according to Plato, was just a notch above tyranny! Plato even declared that democracy is guilty of "never giving a thought to the

---

[3] Daniel R. Ortiz, "The Democratic Paradox of Campaign Finance Reform," *Stanford Law Review* 50:3 (February 1998), pp. 893–914.

pursuits which make a statesman, and promoting to honor any one who professes to be the people's friend."[4]

This skepticism about democracy was echoed by Aristotle (384–322 B.C.E.), another Greek philosopher and a student of Plato. He argued that neither tyranny nor democracy had the best interests or "the common good of all" at heart. Instead, tyranny seeks to further the self-interest of a monarch and democracy seeks to promote only the interests of the "needy."[5] Aristotle believed that an aristocracy was needed to promote the common interests of the society.

Sadly, the electoral process set up by Mr. Krabs turned SpongeBob's good-natured bid for office into something horrific. Thanks to the rigors of the campaign trail, SpongeBob was on track to becoming a tyrant—someone using the people for his own irrational desires. He began to tell them what he thought they wanted to hear so that he could gain power, rather than what they needed to hear so that Bikini Bottom would become a better place.

A Squidward supporter who was jealous of SpongeBob's victory might argue that SpongeBob was inherently a bad candidate, focused on satisfying personal goals such as fame. He was pleased to carry a scepter, have the title of Royal Patty, and have a Krabby Patty named after him. The citizens of Bikini Bottom could rot for all he cared. They could just cast their votes and then disappear. Squidward could argue that SpongeBob was driven by desire and apparently lacking virtue, echoing the sentiments of Plato who was very skeptical about trusting people who wanted to hold office.

In the case of the Krusty Krab, the election was all rigged by the guy behind the scenes, Mr. Krabs. He was

---

4 Plato, *The Republic* (Barnes and Noble, 2004), p. 321.

5 Aristotle, *Politics* (Cosmo, 2008), Book III, p. 12.

focused on baser desires such as trying to get as much money as possible. This tight-clawed individual was the real tyrant. As a member of the corporate elite, he manipulated the election to create wealth for himself. Plato applauds those rulers who have the best interests of society at heart, not those who wield power to line their own shells with money like Mr. Krabs. Mr. Krabs acted as though he was interested in the opinions and preferences of the people, when in reality he had the unjust motivations of simply promoting his own wealth.

A second problem for democracy demonstrated in *SpongeBob* is that the people who win an election are not necessarily prepared for the position they win. I'm sure Plato, being the wise philosopher he was, would have been a SpongeBob fan. But, if the campaign for Royal Krabby were for an actual political office, would Plato have thought SpongeBob was right for the job of Royal Krabby? After all, SpongeBob has a hard enough time passing Boating School. Could he really be fit to lead?

Plato maintained that certain types of people are not meant for government, and that governance should be reserved for those with expertise and proper motivation. He argued that there are three classes of people: Rulers, Auxiliaries, and Producers. The Rulers and Auxiliaries together make up a bigger category called Guardians. These people have specialized functions and should not cross over into another class and interfere with things that do not concern them. Instead they should focus on acting justly in their own sphere of influence. In other words, Krabby Patty flippers should remain Krabby Patty flippers and not try to run for office. This means that the Royal Krabby, if it were a real office, should devote himself to being the Royal Krabby and not meddle in how sea fried onions are produced.

Squidward and SpongeBob are employees at Krusty Krab which puts them into the Producer class. What were they thinking? That they could stop flipping Krabby Patties and become the Royal Krabby? In fairness to Squidward, he really didn't want to run for the position of Royal Krabby. He was just following the orders of his employer and wanted to impress Mr. Krabs.

Plato's followers might argue that SpongeBob had not been properly educated to become a part of the Ruler class. Even if he really was a Ruler at heart, he had not been prepared to be a member of the Ruler class and therefore should not have tried to climb out of the Producer class. He was good at flipping Krabby Patties and should have remained in his place. Ill-informed candidates running for a political office with no preparation would lead to the candidates pandering to the people for votes by giving them all kinds of freedoms and liberties. The people would then get drunk on this liberty and become tyrannical. Political candidates in most democracies never have to take a class or read a book on how to be a ruler or guardian of their society. If you're going to run for political office to rule society, shouldn't this education be way up there (along with watching *SpongeBob*) on your list of priorities?

A third problem with democracy is that the only guarantee is that the most popular person is elected. People might vote based on who is attractive, likeable, warm and compassionate, or even humorous. In fact, research done by political scientists at Massachusetts Institute of Technology found that, regardless of country or cultural context, more attractive candidates tend to fare better in elections that less attractive ones.[6] Mr. Krabs catered to

---

[6] Peter Dizikes, "Looks Like a Winner," *MIT News* (July 21st, 2010), <http://web.mit.edu/newsoffice/2010/candidate-looks-0721.html>.

the masses who were probably only concerned with trying to choose the most attractive candidate. I mean, really— Squidward for Royal Krabby? Have you seen that face? It's no wonder SpongeBob won! But, if it's true that people found SpongeBob more adorable than Squidward and based their vote on this attribute, what does that say about democracy?

A Defense of Democracy

Democracy must not be all bad or else our well-intentioned SpongeBob never would have agreed to an election, right? One defense of democracy comes from British philosopher John Stuart Mill (1806–1873) who strongly upheld the right of people to decide for themselves how they should be governed. Mill declared, "The only freedom which deserves the name is that of pursuing our own good in our own way, so long as we do not attempt to deprive others of theirs, or impede their efforts to obtain it."[7]

Mill definitely would not have wanted to trample upon the ability of the Krusty Krab's customers to choose SpongeBob for Royal Krabby. Plato might have felt that someone should not vote for a member of the Producer class in an election. Mill, however, would have felt that this was blocking the right of the individual to freely choose their candidate. This freedom means that it's okay if we choose a candidate like SpongeBob simply because he's adorable. Having the freedom to make this decision is more important than the outcome of whether or not a competent candidate is selected for a position.

Another benefit of democracy is that it encourages education. Since the people rule, they need to be edu-

---

[7] John Stuart Mill, *On Liberty* (Dover, 2002), p. 56.

cated so they can do their part. Democracy and education go together like Kelp Patties and fried sea-onions. Mill felt education was essential to preserving liberty. While it's true Plato might not like to see a Producer try to become a Ruler, Mill might question what's to hinder a dynamic sponge in a democracy from being educated to become a Ruler. And while Plato declared that a good philosopher and leader should not be someone who learns information and then does not retain it, SpongeBob has demonstrated an ability to learn (and as a sponge soaks knowledge up). In the example where he was trying to fill the air with carbon dioxide to make summer start sooner, he later allowed himself to be educated by his friend Sandy about the dangers of global warming. SpongeBob was able to use Sandy's information to save the climate for everyone in Bikini Bottom.

A third benefit of democracy is that it demonstrates a proper order for society. You don't grab power just because you did a heroic deed. SpongeBob never tried to claim title as Ruler for his efforts against global warming although he did keep his title of pool manager. The beautiful community and the natural summer weather that resulted showed he had Bikini Bottom's true interests at heart. SpongeBob's efforts were so successful that even Mr. Krabs began trying to do his part to help the community by giving restaurant discounts to customers who made their way to the Krusty Krab without a vehicle. However, SpongeBob didn't claim to rule Bikini Bottom after this heroism. It wouldn't be proper in a democracy.

A fourth benefit of democracy is that it encourages public service—people putting the good of others above their own interests. Democracy is based on the idea that the people rule. Therefore, all people in a democracy can act like Plato's Guardians of that society because they have a stake in seeking the common good. They are not forcibly serving some dictator, but are themselves valued members of society. What amazes me about SpongeBob is that such a natural leader and a bright and shining example of a perfect citizen has such a lack of self-interest.

The Ideal Candidate

One time, Plankton came into town to try to steal the Krabby Patty formula. Sinister Squid, Ugly Urchin, Bad Blowfish, and Ghastly Grouper were just several of the creepy guys who came to town with Plankton. These tough guys were so bad even the cops fled town. Not only did they try to steal the formula, they also car-jacked an ice cream truck and even ran away after ringing a doorbell. To top it off, they even began to "pop bubble wrap in the library!" Horror of horrors!!![8] And, although his job description only included flipping patties, SpongeBob went far above and beyond his minimum-wage duties to save Bikini Bottom from the low-life scum that began to infest town. Using a huge jelly-fishing net, SpongeBob put a stop to the crimes of the bad guys and saved the day. Everyone returned to town once SpongeBob had restored order.

Aristotle believed that, although it was imperfect, representative democracy had the potential to allow a variety of interests to coexist within the same society. He called this type of system a "polity" to distinguish it from the downsides of democracy. In a democracy, the majority of people rule with the goal of seeking their own interests. In a polity, "the citizens at large administer the state for the common interest" (*Politics*, Book III). SpongeBob would therefore be an ideal candidate in a potential Bikini

---

[8] Sarah Willson, *Man Sponge Saves the Day* (Simon and Schuster, 2009).

Bottom representative democracy because he displayed his capacity to look out for the interests of everyone even when it didn't serve his own immediate interests.

Although he never receives more compensation than the gratitude of the other citizens along with his minimum-wage salary, SpongeBob willingly works hard to make Bikini Bottom the best place on Earth. If you ever have the chance to be a "Guardian," or to choose the Guardian of your society, I hope you'll be as wise as my favorite sponge.

9
I'm the King. That's What I Do

Adam Barkman

Near the beginning of *The SpongeBob SquarePants Movie*, King Neptune is about to execute the royal crown polisher for simply doing his job. When asked by his daughter Mindy why he has "to be so mean," Neptune replies, "I'm the king. That's what I do." But is this really so? Do kings really have to be cruel and ruthless? How are they distinguishable from tyrants? Indeed, what should a king be like—what is his character and what are his duties?

Executing Poles and Other Wrong Acts

Dante Aligheri (1265–1321) begins his *De Monarchia* ('On Monarchy') by claiming, "All men whose higher nature has endowed them with a love of truth obviously have the greatest interest in working for future generations."

Dante assumes from the very outset the existence of truth, which was obvious to many of our forebears but not as obvious to us nowadays. For Dante, truth is an objective quality. It's really out there and, in some measure, can be discerned by the human mind. For instance, we say the propositions "1 + 1 = 2" or "It's always wrong to torture a child for fun" are true, not because they're merely our subjective opinions, but because these opinions, which presumably are held for the right reasons, have a rightness or correspondence with deeper reality.

This reality, for Dante, is first God Himself (thus, $1 + 1 = 2$ is primarily an idea in God's mind and it's true because it's grounded in God's unchanging nature) and second God's creational or natural laws (God issues commands, based on His unchanging nature and ideas, and these commands, such as "it's always wrong to torture a child for fun," require obedience in creatures). We could even say that truth is a kind of justice—it's the quality that obtains when we treat each thing, person, or circumstance as it ought to be treated (this is the definition of justice which I will be using throughout, though obviously it's not the only possible definition).

So, when King Neptune tries to execute a pole he happens to bump into (in *The SpongeBob SquarePants movie*), his behavior isn't right because it doesn't correspond with how people should act. Neptune isn't behaving justly because treating each thing as it ought to be treated means not holding things responsible for actions that they didn't do.

Behavior Befitting a King

According to Dante (also author of *The Divine Comedy*, arguably the greatest piece of literature in the history of the world), kingship is primarily a matter of God's choice (*De Monarchia*, 3.16). The way Dante sees it, King Neptune, though a god (lower case "g"), would still have been created by God (capital "G"). In this way, Dante would likely argue that King Neptune, just like Augustus Caesar, was "ordained by nature for rule" (*De Monarchia*, 2.6), while others, such as Patrick and Plankton, were not.

This isn't to say that Patrick and Plankton were made for no purpose—far from it. It's only to say that Neptune was made to rule, while the other sea creatures were made for other tasks, such as comedy or invention. This, in fact, perhaps makes Neptune partially right to imprison his negligent son, Triton, since it's at least true that the boy needed to "learn to embrace his destiny" (Season 7, Episode 126, "The Clash of Triton"). Moreover, we could even see the female fish's exclamation upon hearing that King Neptune will be eating at the Krusty Krab "I'm a huge fan of the royal family. I just love everything they do" as demonstrating people's God-given love of hierarchy.

In other words, respect for the royal family is evidence, albeit weak evidence, that kingship is God-ordained and therefore good in and of itself. Particular kings might abuse their power or be corrupt but that hardly invalidates the goodness of the form, idea, or original creational design of kingship, just as we wouldn't say that the Krabbie Patty itself is bad just because one particular patty happened to be on the grill too long.

Nowadays many might see this blatant theory of hierarchy as inherently unjust. But here we must be careful. Justice, as I'm using the term in this essay, means treating each thing or person as it, he, or she ought to be treated—that is, according to their unique natures. But, according to Dante, God Himself made the natures of all created things and so justice means treating a king as a king, comedy as comedy, and so on. In other words, those who think it unfair that God made Neptune king are actually the ones who are promoting unfair or unjust behavior because they want to treat a king as if he weren't one. This is why in the Bible David didn't kill King Saul, an evil ruler by all accounts, saying that it isn't right "to raise a hand against the LORD's anointed" (1 Samuel 24:6).

Nevertheless, Dante isn't oblivious to the fragment of truth in this objection. That's why he labors to show, with some dubious reasoning, that those whom God chooses to rule will demonstrate, in their actions, that they were supposed to rule. Using the Romans as his example, Dante argues that: 1. kings and emperors should rule for the good of all people; 2. the Roman emperors ruled, at least better than anyone else, for the good of all people; 3. therefore, the Romans were God's political elect (*De Monarchia*, 2.5).

Leaving aside the most questionable proposition, #3 (the conclusion to his argument), Dante, who's following Plato and Aristotle here, seems correct in maintaining that kings or political rulers ought to be servants of the people: they ought to be thinking of the good of all those below them. In other words, if a king wants to live up to his name and nature and not simply be a tyrant, he must act justly and part of doing so means serving his people. Hence Queen Amphitrite is correct when she says to the mopey Neptune, "Surely this isn't the behavior befitting a king—hiding in bed for days on end, doing nothing but watching daytime television!" (Season 7, Episode 126, "The Clash of Triton"), but must be an active servant of the people. Thus, Princess Mindy is right when she asks her Dad, "Where is your love and compassion?" (*The SpongeBob SquarePants Movie*).

Nevertheless, serving the people is only one part of what it means for a king to act justly or according to his nature. The other part, that which must be paired with service, is the assertion of strength and authority. A king, in other words, must be able to judge his people and make important decisions that will affect, sometimes unpleasantly, those below him. In this way, Neptune isn't wrong for referring to the people of Bikini Bottom as "my . . . flock," nor for seeing the need for some "smiting" ("The Clash of Triton").

You Won't Be the King until You Learn To . . .

To talk about serving people and exercising strength is to talk very narrowly about the duties of kingship, and, indeed, it's to get ahead of the ball. To be a proper or just king, one must first be a proper or just person.

Now men, gods, and talking sponges all have one important thing in common: they're rational souls; they have been created, Dante would say, with intellect and free will. They act justly or properly when, in this bare sense, they act according to their nature, which is to say when they act rationally (*De Monarchia*, 1.3). Following a Christian appropriation of Plato and Aristotle, Dante believed that the first thing a rational soul or person realizes when he acts rationally is that people were made for happiness (*De Monarchia*, 1.4). And even though many—perhaps most—people will be mistaken about what constitutes their happiness (due to limited knowledge and sin), all in fact want happiness, which, for rational souls, is the realization of our true self.

Because God created all things, our true self can only be realized by finding it in God, the Creator. Therefore, the more rational a person is the more he will seek out God. What he discovers along the way is that if he wants to draw close to God, he needs to act justly, for God is the source of all Justice. Indeed, if he wants to be in perfect fellowship with God, thus discovering his true nature and destiny, he needs to have a nature that is like God's, for no injustice can enter into the presence that is burning holiness of God. Even SpongeBob knows that only if he becomes an immortal could he live in Atlantis as Neptune's fry cook (Season 1, Episode 19b, "The Golden Spatula"). Thus, acquiring—mostly, if not completely, by God's grace—a virtuous character is necessary in order to be a properly functioning person.

Four Virtues

As a typical medieval thinker, Dante believed that a virtuous character is made up of at least seven virtues: four cardinal virtues (prudence, courage, temperance, and justice) and three theological ones (faith, hope, and love). Needless to say, a king worthy of his name will possess these to a very high degree and certainly more than the average person.

Prudence, the first virtue, is practical, but not pragmatic, wisdom. A king must understand God's laws relevant to politics and be aware of how to apply his knowledge to particular problems that arise. In this way, he's supremely practical, but isn't pragmatic since pragmatism, denying or leaving aside any question of objective truth and right, asserts only what works.

Plankton is the most pragmatic one in Bikini Bottom, for he will do whatever it takes to acquire the recipe for the Krabby Patty. A prudent ruler will always endeavor to find ways to achieve the goals of politics, namely, to secure the rights, freedom, and security of the people, but never at the cost of violating God's natural, moral laws. Nearly every medieval political theorist, including Dante, understood the servant aspect of being a king to mean securing justice, freedom and peace for the king's subjects.

As a wise man, the king will remember that he is below God and responsible to God for the well-being of the people underneath him. Because he is wise, he understands that he must be a servant-leader; he knows when to be generous and when to be firm. In "The Clash of Triton," Neptune shows some understanding of the need for this balance (thus, he tells Triton, "Son, I understand if you want to keep me locked up in this cage, but . . . release these others for they are innocent"); however, for the most part, Neptune is imprudent, typically seeing "smiting" as the solution to every political problem.

Courage is the virtue that controls the passionate part of the soul. It's what moves people to act in the face of fear or laziness. This virtue is vital for all people, but especially for rulers, since a good, but cowardly, politician will never be able to act upon his convictions. Dante quotes approvingly a passage from the old epic poem the *Aeneid*, where Aeneas, the father of the Romans, is told, "You are to impose the ways of peace, sparing those who submit and being inexorable to the proud." In other words, kings must be courageous; they must be unafraid of establishing the common good.

Triton, Neptune's hippy son, began as a prince who cared about the people, going so far as to discover a cure for "all mortal diseases." Nevertheless, Neptune, passionately denounced him, saying, "How many times do I have to tell you? We are gods—we don't have diseases nor do we care whether or not the mortals contract them!" ("The Clash of Triton").

On the one hand, Neptune has courage to enforce his political convictions, but sadly they are misguided ones: he has courage but little prudence. On the other hand, Triton has some prudence (his priorities of service to his people shows wisdom), but has no courage to stand up for what is right: he has prudence but no courage. Needless to say, a king worthy of his name must have both virtues.

Temperance is the virtue of self-control. It's the habit in the soul that, following the guidance of wisdom, uses the passionate part of the soul to control the appetitive part. In plainer language, temperance is the strength of will that not only resists temptation (as courage does) but goes further and pacifies the hungers of the appetite (for food, drink, sex, power, and so on) to such a degree that there is harmony within the soul. The self-controlled man is one at peace with himself. The self-controlled king is at peace with himself and so can, without desiring power or money or fame, dedicate himself to his political office. Neither Neptune, nor his son, Triton, appear to be at peace with themselves—both are whimsical and temperamental—and so could hardly be free from the temptations that arise with kingship. Were Mindy Neptune's son, and not his daughter, she would make a superior ruler since she shows herself to be level-headed and slow to anger.

Why couldn't Mindy become the ruler of the land instead of Triton? She is female and hence isn't spiritually qualified to lead men. The Christian tradition has always maintained that gender is far from an accidental or unimportant thing. In the Bible, God declares Himself masculine, and since God is a spirit, most theologians assume that gender is a spiritual quality. Moreover, since God has authority over all things, there's a strong connection between masculinity and authority. That's why the Bible makes husbands the "heads" or leaders of their wives, and also why orthodox Christianity has always opposed priestesses in the Church (Seven hundred years after Dante, his Roman Catholic Church still very much insists on this point).

All virtues are such because they demonstrate what's just. For example, the wise man is he who knows many true things and is aware of how to apply these truths to particular situations. He knows what a thing is and what to do with that thing, and treats each thing as it ought to be treated. The courageous woman knows when to act and when not to and then seeks the proper action. And finally, the man of temperance is one who possesses a soul that functions harmoniously. Thus, we can see that justice touches all aspects of life, not least the political aspect. So a king must be just and fair, acting properly in each situation and treating all things and persons as they ought to be treated; this requires wisdom, courage, and temperance.

When Neptune punishes SpongeBob for Patrick's hostile words—"Your friend's arrogance will cost you dearly!" (Season 1, Episode 19b, "The Golden Spatula"), he acts unjustly since Patrick alone should be punished for his disrespectful behavior. Moreover, when Neptune initially fails to keep his promise to make the one who can draw the golden spatula his royal fry cook, he is, as SpongeBob says, "a liar," which is to say, an unjust person, since justice requires that promises be kept—that oaths be treated like oaths, namely, as ethical contracts that, all things considered, must be upheld.

And Three More

Those are the four cardinal virtues, but what about the theological ones? Dante was a Christian political thinker and as such thought that the king is primarily chosen by God. Accordingly, the king—at least with the advent of Christ—should be a Christian one, and that means, among other things, that he demonstrates faith, hope, and love both as a person and as a king.

Faith is pretty straightforward—but tell that to the theologians! As a virtue it has to do with being aware of God's existence and something of His nature. This isn't blind belief—far from it. It's specially revealed facts or knowledge that God, by His grace, instills in certain people. For example, at one point SpongeBob didn't know how to get to Shell City, but once he was told this information by the divine Mindy, he now had a new set of facts—new knowledge—to reason with and from (*The SpongeBob Squarepants Movie*). The same's true of the Christian who has been given a new set of facts about God and His plans. Thus, the man, and king, of faith is he who knows a number of things about God. This is vital to kingship since ignorance of

God and His ways will always lead to poor practical political solutions.

For example, if Neptune were aware of God and
something of His nature, he'd know that since God is
a—indeed, the—just king, he, too, ought to be a just
king. Faith, in other words, would give Neptune knowledge about how he ought to act as one under God's
authority.

Hope must be distinguished from a wish. Hope is the
rational desire to find one's true self in the presence of
one's creator; it's the desire for true happiness, for God,
who is a real person. A wish is something that a person
wants but can't actually get. In its worst form it is a kind of
wish-fulfillment or neurosis. When SpongeBob says to
Patrick, "I hope to see you at the party," we know that it's
a real possibility that SpongeBob could see Patrick at the
party. He could, if things worked out, really see Patrick
there. However, when SpongBob says of Patrick, "I wish I
were you," he asserts something that is no longer a possibility. He can't really be Patrick.

By faith—rational knowledge of God's existence—
people can know that God exists, and thus it is a rational
or real possibility to find one's true self in God. Hope is
the rational desire for this real possibility. All people, but
especially kings, need this virtue since without the desire
to find one's true self—without a desire for the truth of
the matter—a person will fall into the temptation to create oneself, to do whatever one likes, ignoring the deeper
reality behind things. Dante again praises Aeneas because
he sought "the divine pleasure by waging a single combat"
(*De Monarchia*, 2.10). In other words, King Aeneas had his
eyes set on the Heavens and thus, because his priorities
were correct, was given kingship on Earth as a bonus. King
Neptune, on the other hand, never set his eyes above, nor
inclines his heart to, anything but his own private con-

cerns (attending house parties and so on), and so understandably is a wayward ruler (Season 3, Episode 51, "House Party").

Love, the last but greatest of the virtues, is the inclination to act on the knowledge acquired by faith. It's the movement of the will to value God and His commandments above all else. As with all the virtues, it's a kind of justice: it's the desire to treat God and His commandments as He and they ought to be treated. Nevertheless, it's also important to distinguish love and justice in that while justice means treating each thing as it ought to be treated, love means going beyond this, treating each thing with more consideration—in a positive sense—than is required.

A just king will treat a solider as a soldier, not wasting them in battle, valuing them for their own sakes and so on, but will also see that he, as king, is politically more valuable than a common solider. Thus, if it came down to a choice between the king sacrificing his own life for one of his soldiers, the just king wouldn't do it. However, the king who possess the virtue of love and mercy, which in Shakespeare's phrase, "seasons justice," will not only be willing but will insist on giving his own life for his soldier (Shakespeare, *Measure for Measure* , Act 4, Scene 1). The king of love, in other words, fights next to his troops; mingles and suffers with his people; and demonstrates self-less consideration to all. Neptune rarely shows love for his subjects and so is a king "unseasoned."

Yours Is Superior, therefore I Concede to You?

Using King Neptune as my example and Dante as my guide, I have looked at the character and duties of a king. A king must be a good or virtuous (mer)man. For this reason, he needs to acquire at least seven virtues: prudence, courage, temperance, justice, faith, hope, and love.

After this, the king must be aware of what it specifically means to be king, namely, being aware of the specifics of the public square. Although King Neptune, and his son Triton each possess some of the virtues, neither have enough to be considered good persons and neither have enough knowledge of politics to be, in a specific sense, good rulers.

Should they, then, be deposed? Should Neptune follow SpongeBob around and serve as his lackey since SpongeBob makes superior patties? ("The Golden Spatula"). Dante would probably say no, calling for Neptune's reform instead. However, each of us must answer this question in our own way.

10

Mr. Krabs's Secret Recipe

Michael Dodge

Seeing SpongeBob SquarePants gleefully flipping Krabby Patties, it's easy to gloss over the deeper issues surrounding Bikini Bottom's favorite fast-food treat. Indeed, much of the comic relief of SpongeBob can be attributed to Sheldon Plankton's nefarious attempts to pilfer Krabs's "secret recipe." Poor Plankton has a hard time with his own struggling Chum Bucket, and his professional and financial failures could all be alleviated by simply knowing how Mr. Krabs makes his Patties. We wonder, then, should Krabs be more charitable with the mischievous little copepod?

What grants Krabs the legal right to guard his property with such gusto? Is it even correct to say Krabs that has an individual right to the secret recipe? By hoarding the secret to the deliciousness of fast-seafood, is Krabs denying a public benefit to Bikini Bottom and violating the notion of collectivist property?

Consumerism and capitalist endeavor resonate with many modern societies, and the jurisprudential (referring to the philosophy of law) and ethical nature of property rights are steadfastly implicated by Krabs's business strategy. Krabs certainly believes he has the right to protect himself from corporate espionage. After all, without that right, his riches would decline.

Two philosophers concerned with questions of rights and property, Thomas Hobbes (1588–1679) and John Locke (1632–1704) would agree that Krabs has a right to his property, albeit for differing reasons. Whereas Hobbes argues that it is social authority that promotes and preserves the right to property, and that this is the only thing that keeps Mr. Krabs from defending his property solely by force, Locke suggests that Krabs's (or, rather, SpongeBob's) labor has caused something of himself to mix with his product, and that this thereby imparts a right to the secret recipe irrespective of what society might think.

Some legal philosophers, like John Rawls (1921–2002), argue that property is not even a proper philosophical target but, rather, a tangential issue to identifying what constitutes a just society. No matter how you catch the jellyfish, the nature of property has been subjected to much philosophical debate.

The (Bikini) Bottom Line—Kinds of Property in SpongeBob's World

Property is essentially a resource, and as such, it may take the form of a solid piece of land such as the Goo Lagoon; buildings or structures built upon land, such as SpongeBob's pineapple-esque home; or even items that one may utilize for trade or pleasure, such as Squidward's clarinet or Patrick's lifetime supply of strawberry bubblegum. Property is a wide-ranging term for resources that form the foundation of society and recreation in many of the world's civilizations, Bikini Bottom among them.

Three identifiable kinds of property are those of collective property, communal property, and private property. Collective property is that which is designed to serve a particular purpose for the public as a whole. The primary component of this property is that the community divides the resources available according to a societal plan. An example would be a religious community that dictates which members are given which resources to perform a task or fulfill a goal set by everyone involved in the decision making of that society. If SpongeBob, Squidward, and Patrick (okay, maybe just SpongeBob and Patrick) decided to form a community distinct from that of the rest of Bikini Bottom, they could collectively decide which resources they had available that would be given to each member of the commune.

Historically, the idea of a five-year plan for resource distribution and economic development has found credence in countries ranging from the former Soviet Union to China and India, among others. Part of the reasoning behind this is the philosophical belief that the resources of any given area, being limited, must be subjected to the will of the individuals affected. Some individuals have moral objections to being told what they can and cannot do with the resources around them unless those same individuals are given some input in the decision making process. Such planning can be done from anything as small as a village town-hall meeting, to a national assembly enacting legislation.

Communal property is that which belongs to everyone, or at least to anyone in an area capable of accessing and utilizing the resource. It differs from collective property in that it is not usually subjected to division for the particular use by individuals in the society. The most common examples are public parks, beaches like Goo Lagoon, or the always fantastic Jellyfish Fields. Commons also differ from private property, since no one may attempt to purchase, sell, barter, or modify (without public consent) that which has been set aside for the common use of all. In *SpongeBob SquarePants*, the commons tend to operate as they properly should. SpongeBob can be seen happily romping around Jellyfish Fields, often accompanied by Patrick, scooping up the jellies as they swim around. Sometimes the jellies are cooperative ("Ditching"), whereas other times they are a bit obstinate and hazardous to Squidward's health ("Jellyfishing").

Jellyfish Fields serves as an example of a rather large commons, since they seem to stretch on and on, having little definite ending. In the air-breathing world, commons are typically not quite so large. Indeed, commons often exist because there is a general lack of available land or resources for any given user. The benefit of the commons is that every user can use the property for his or her own benefit without having to collect, create, or expend the necessary capital to purchase an individual plot of land for exclusive use. Since there are many individuals incapable of purchasing large tracts of land (such as poor boating class students or simply the general populace), commons look like a good and convenient type of property.

But we can't overlook the specter of the infamous "tragedy of the commons." The tragedy of the commons demonstrates that rational and logical behavior can, at times, actually produce an irrational result. Classically, the tragedy of the commons involves a scenario whereby a group of ranchers are able to share a piece of land on which they can support their cattle. Each farmer must spend his resources and take care of his property wisely, and he must bear his own costs. However, because the maintenance of the land is a burden shared by all the ranchers, any given rancher recognizes that if he puts one more head of cattle on the land, he will reap all the benefits of the additional animal, but everyone who uses the land will bear the burden of the overgrazing this causes to the commons.

The rancher rationally behaves in a manner to maximize his own wealth, whilst enjoying the lowered costs that consequentially result. Unfortunately, if one assumes each rancher is capable of equally rational behavior, each individual will add more and more cattle to the field, knowing that all the others will share the cost, but not share in the benefits. Collectively, these actions are highly irrational, since in the end the overgrazing will negatively affect everyone, eventually destroying the property.

Similar tragedies can result from an increase in the number of people using the commons, rather than simply increasing their use by those already present. In Bikini Bottom, Jellyfish Fields could be the common property at issue. If SpongeBob, Patrick, and perhaps even Squidward are frolicking away with a day of jellyfishing, the commons will likely suffer no harm. On the other hand, when Krabs over-exploits the jellyfish to maximize his personal profit in "Jellyfish Hunter," the capacity of the property to serve the needs of any given individual was threatened. Overusing Jellyfish Fields could permanently damage the land or scare off or drastically deplete the jellyfish population, and then the tragedy has been realized.

While the debate over the likelihood of a tragedy of the commons being created may be as much economic as philosophical, the issue remains interesting to philosophy because of how it may affect the distribution of wealth and the ability to earn a living for oneself, each of which affect the notions of a just society and of personal dignity—applicable to humans, sponges, sea stars, and megalomaniacal single-celled organisms alike.[1]

---

[1] See Garret Hardin, "The Tragedy of the Commons," *Science* (December 13th, 1968).

Avast . . . This Is Plankton! Stealing Me Booty!

The tragedy of the commons is a possibility that some argue makes a rational case for the third kind of property found in Bikini Bottom—private property. One might argue that the tragedy of the commons doesn't mean that privatizing property is the proper course, and that perhaps the Bikini Bottom police force should more adequately enforce safeguards to prevent its occurrence. On the other hand, the injustice of the tragedy of the commons might be averted by the creation or recognition of private property (like Krabs's booty). Perhaps the most familiar kind of property, private property gives an individual nearly complete control over the resource in question; be it land, the fruits derived from it, or any of a number of other goods or items. Thus, SpongeBob owns his pineapple under the sea, Squidward owns his Easter Island head home, Plankton owns the Chum Bucket, and Mr. Krabs owns the Krusty Krab.

The Scottish philosopher David Hume (1711–1776) observed that there were four ways that property originated, all of which directly concern private property. In his *Treatise of Human Nature*, Hume pointed out that property can arise from occupation, prescription, accession, or succession.[2]

Occupation is the simplest concept, whereby an individual or individuals occupy a piece of land, or take possession of some object, and claim that it now belongs to them. While this sounds like a childish method of property acquisition, it actually has a strong historical tradition, and even legal backing, to an extent.

---

[2] David Hume, *Treatise of Human Nature* (1739), in *Philosophical Works*, (1964).

Prescription is akin to a title that has property attached to it, and would be seen most often in situations where, for example, King Neptune will eventually pass his crown and property on to Triton. Accession is the process by which someone may enjoy the fruits that arise from the property itself, as where Krabs enjoys the profit from the Krabby Patties sold in his restaurant, or if Sandy Cheeks wants to pick some acorns off of her tree for a light snack. The final method is succession, where one generation leaves its property to the natural inheritors of that property, such as Pearl Krabs eventually inheriting the Krusty Krab.

Private property provides the most power for the individual who possesses it. In philosophy of law, property is sometimes discussed under "bundle theory"; the idea that property rights are like a bundle of sticks—there're multiple rights associated with ownership of the property, and just as in a bundle of sticks, some may be added or taken away, so long as the bundle more or less remains intact.

Thus, Sandy may use her land to build a productivity maximizing machine ("Overbooked"), and may start and stop work on this or any other project without the approval or consent of SpongeBob, Patrick, or Squidward. Sandy may decide when her employees can and cannot work, and whether and when they are allowed access to her Treedome. The practical realities of the modern world must allow from some proscriptions to the absolute power theoretically associated with private property (labor laws may protect worker exploitation, and Sandy cannot use her property in such as way as to be a nuisance to her neighbors).[3]

---

[3] Another limitation is the principle of eminent domain, where a governmental body may forcibly take private property for the sake of a public need (such as for a boating school), though the owner must be justly compensated.

Krabby Patties and the Just Society

Much of the discourse on the philosophy of property centers on the view that property is necessary for the establishment and maintenance of a just and civil society. The English philosopher Thomas Hobbes made a study of property in his *De Cive*, noting that his first task in analyzing human nature was to identify what constituted the idea of something being 'mine' as opposed to someone else's. Hobbes noted that individuals naturally entered into the world with needs, and that these became satisfied by the creation and protection of property. In this way people could provide for themselves, and this was simultaneously the source of division among the populace. People would create divisions as to where one individual's property ended, and where the next began. These very divisions gave rise to the law, since without its efforts, individuals would be forced to defend what was theirs by their strength alone, which helps little when a larger, more powerful brute comes along to take what belongs to you (think of Larry the Lobster trying to take the Chum Bucket from Plankton—the latter's puny strength would be easily overcome by the muscular life guard).

A just society, then, depends on the creation and enforcement of the law to protect property rights. Hobbes noted that "every man hath his proper Right . . . whereby we may know what is properly ours, what another man's; so as others may not hinder us from the free use and enjoyment of our own; and we may not interrupt others in the quiet possession of theirs."[4] The state is the natural organ to enforce such rights, since the law would be meaningless if those possessing superior strength didn't enforce it. The law can order Plankton to

---

[4] Thomas Hobbes, *De Cive* (epistolary dedicatory).

cease his futile attempts at pilfering the Krabby Patty secret recipe, but if the Bikini Bottom police and Judge Trout did not stand ready to enforce the rule, it would be all for naught.

John Locke shared with Hobbes the view that property arose naturally. In *Two Treatises of Government*, Locke proposes a story to explain the origins of property (adapted here to an account under the sea). Imagine that King Neptune has just created Bikini Bottom, and needs to populate it. He zaps his lightning from one location to another, filling his new world with SpongeBob, Patrick, Sandy, Squidward, Plankton, and many others. Finding themselves in a state of nature, they all naturally claim the resources around them to feed and clothe themselves, which begins the state of ownership.

As Locke wrote, "He that is nourished by the acorns he picked up under an oak . . . has certainly appropriated them to himself. Nobody can deny but the nourishment is his."[5] (Sandy Cheeks would certainly agree.) In appropriating these resources, the denizens of Bikini Bottom thereby modify and improve them. In the process, they impart something of themselves into the property, which both gives them a moral justification for protecting their property, and helps to form their personal identity.

Krabs labors to create the perfect, delicious, juicy Krabby Patties that delight all of Bikini Bottom, and his very identity is transparently bound to his product. You might be tempted to argue that it's SpongeBob doing all the "laboring" to create the perfect patty, but recall the very first episode, "Help Wanted," where SpongeBob seeks to work at the Krusty Krab because of his love of the

---

[5] John Locke, *Two Treatises of Government* (1689), in *Works* (1832), p. 354.

Krabby Patty. Likewise, "The Original Fry Cook" makes us aware of cooks working in Krabs's kitchen long before SpongeBob arrived.

This identification of Krabs with his goods and source of income, and therefore his ability to support himself, is the moral and legal justification for Krabs's efforts to thwart the machinations of his plucky, single-minded competitor. Krabs is able to sell his patties to all who desire them, thereby improving the lot of society by creating both markets for other goods (the companies that provide him cups, dishes, buns, fries, etc.), satisfying needs of others for nutrition, and increasing the overall happiness of the society. While Locke's philosophy tends to support the classical liberal idea of free market economies, he is aware that this form of distribution can create inequalities. There are the Squilliam Fancysons and Krabs of the world, and then there are the Squidwards and Planktons.

The law is designed to protect property from the envy, greed, and criminal acts that follow in the wake of this system. Justice arises as a means of preserving property, for without it anarchy would rule. A simple example reveals itself in the chaos experienced by SpongeBob, Patrick, and Squidward in "Pineapple Fever." Attempting to weather a storm ravaging Bikini Bottom, the fated trio entertain themselves with various games until Squidward can stand SpongeBob and Patrick's shenanigans no longer.

Squidward creates a new game ruled by but one law—no one can cross the chalk line once it's been drawn. Congratulating himself on his ingenious maneuver, Squidward begins to think he'll be able to sit out the storm in peace, untroubled by SpongeBob and Patrick—after all, they can't cross the chalk line. Hunger, however, compels Squidward to attempt to cross his own line and break the law of the game. This causes the entire household to descend into anarchy in a battle over the contents of the refrigerator. Squidward asks: "Is this really what we've come to? Is one little storm all it takes to turn us into complete animals?" Hobbes and Locke argue that individuals would be little more than such animals without the protection of the law.

Hume also holds that property is natural to humanity. He recognizes that individuals live in a world which provides them with a great mind, and that this mind is capable of realizing the exceptional limits on the resources available to them. Thus, individuals like Plankton and Krabs realize that the resources they need are not infinite, and they must compete to obtain them. Unlike Locke, Hume doesn't focus on the idea that in the beginning, individuals found themselves in a state of nature where nothing belonged to anyone before each individual acquired her own property. Hume recognizes that individuals' needs have caused them to squirrel away what they can to provide for themselves, and that society can only exist if everyone respects the integrity of property rights. He points out that people come to realize that it is in each other's interest to not interfere with another's property.

Hume also differs from Locke in arguing that the relationship of property to its owner is not a natural one, but a moral one. In fact, Hume argues that if anything about human nature is certain, it's that "it is only from the selfishness and confin'd generosity of men, along with scanty provision nature has made for his wants, that justice derives its origin."[6] Justice exists as a function of property rights.

Hume recognizes that protecting property will result in unequal distribution of goods between individuals, but

---

6 David Hume, *Treatise of Human Nature* (1739), in *Philosophical Works* (1964), pp. 263–64, 267–68.

that this is necessarily better than any alternative. While he focuses on selfishness as a motive for acquiring property (à la Plankton), he also knows that people are capable of generosity (à la Patrick, as when he gave five ultra-rare Mermaid Man and Barnacle Boy trading cards to SpongeBob in "The Card").

Unfortunately, selfishness and other negative motivations would take over without the power of law to stand in the way. Forget Plankton's mind-controlling devices—if the law did not protect property rights, then "society must immediately dissolve, and everyone must fall into that savage and solitary condition, which is infinitely worse than the worst situation that can possibly be suppos'd in society" (p. 269). In this way, protecting property is advantageous to the whole civilization. Self-interest may be the motivation for Krabs's right to have his property protected, but the same rules that protect him protect all other citizens too.

Ultimately, individuals are concerned first with their own welfare, and with that of their family and closest friends. They will occupy themselves with acquiring the resources they need to serve those interests before they dream of creating great buildings, works of art, scientific wonders, or recreational trivialities. Thus, property rights, protected by legal and ethical standards, provide the foundation for individuals to focus less on simple needs, and more on the evolution and advancement of a society governed by a slew of other laws and regulations; without them civilization as we know it could not exist.

No Matter How You Flip the Patty . . .

Regardless of which property scheme is employed by a society—collective, communal, or private—property rights are a source of much philosophical debate. Locke,

Hume, and Hobbes would surely defend Krabs's right to protect his formula from the evil schemes of Plankton, since such a right is a foundational value for a just society.

Communal property proponents might claim that food (such as the Krabby Patty) is a public good, and that the profits derived from the Krusty Krab should be distributed in an equitable fashion, thereby preventing the social and economic inequalities that often result from private-property systems. True justice, they could say, would not produce such disparate outcomes for the members of a society.

Would a commons be better? If all of the resources of Bikini Bottom were available for anyone to claim, and private property forbidden or strictly controlled, would the Krabby Patty ever have been created? The reality is that Krabs does have a legal and moral right to keep his Krabby Patty recipe secret, even if his personal motivations are selfish. Plankton will continue to try, and likely fail, to discover the formula, but Judge Trout, the Bikini Bottom police, and his own ineptitudes will forever be there to stop him.

11
Nautical Nonsense and Naturalism

GREG AHRENHOERSTER

SpongeBob SquarePants is, of course, an aquatic animal (my wife, a former high-school biology teacher, assures me that sponges are animals). His friends and neighbors are also animals—a starfish, a squirrel, an octopus, and a crab, to name a few. Yet in the animated television series that bears his name, SpongeBob and his friends are clearly not representatives of nature. They are, despite their silliness, quite civilized.

They live in the urban center of Bikini Bottom; they watch television; they have jobs; they drive motorized vehicles (or in SpongeBob's case, aspire to drive one). However, "nature" in a more traditional sense is present in the world of SpongeBob, and the citizens of Bikini Bottom have a complex relationship with it, just as human beings do. In a few episodes, SpongeBob and his friends get lost in the undersea wilderness (once, for example, while SpongeBob and Squidward are trying to deliver a pizza and another time when SpongeBob and Patrick sneak along on Sandy's camping trip), but most often nature is represented by the jellyfish that SpongeBob lovingly chases through Jellyfish Fields.

SpongeBob's Place in Literary History (in Regards to Nature)

Humankind's relationship with nature is one that has been long explored in literature, with nature at various times being presented as being the home of dark magic, thus a place to be feared, as shown by the "Weird Sisters" in William Shakespeare's (1564–1616) *Macbeth* (or, if you prefer, the supernatural Flying Dutchman who harasses Mr. Krabs when he's lost at sea in "SpongeBob vs. The Big One").

Other times, in the tradition of pastoral poetry, nature is presented as a welcome escape from the corruption of "the court" or civilization—an innocent place where humans are free to philosophize or woo, as the case may be, without the usual political or social demands that occupy our lives. This is seen, for example, in Shakespeare's *As You Like It*, in which most of the characters escape a corrupt court by going into the peaceful Forest of Arden, where almost everyone falls in love. In the play, nature even magically transforms the evil Duke Frederick when he goes into the wilderness after the others; in a remarkable plot twist, he suddenly decides to go off and live as a monk, giving the Dukedom back to its proper ruler, Duke Senior, and allowing the others (most of them, at least) to return to their lives at court. A SpongeBob parallel might be SpongeBob and a temporarily transformed Plankton skipping through a field of flowers singing the "F.U.N. Song."

In both *As You Like It* and "F.U.N." these forays into nature must only be temporary as duty calls the characters back to civilization (ruling the country or flipping Krabby Patties, as the case may be). In Shakespeare plays, nature is a nice place to visit, but you wouldn't want to live there.

These two seemingly contradictory presentations of nature (as dangerous and innocent) dominated literature into the middle of the nineteenth century, when Transcendentalists like Ralph Waldo Emerson (1803–1882) and Henry David Thoreau (1817–1862) painted an even more idealistic picture of nature, as a place to go to find spirituality and happiness that were being destroyed by the industrialization of society.

At its core, Transcendentalism was a religious and philosophical rebellion, with Transcendentalists expressing resistance to the growing scientific emphasis on physical evidence, giving preference to a more spiritual aspect of humanity and the idea that all people had access to divine inspiration if they simply looked for it. Often, Transcendentalists argued that this spirituality could be found in nature. Probably the best-known example of a Transcendentalist text about humanity's relationship with nature is Thoreau's book *Walden, or Life in the Woods*, which describes two years Thoreau spent living in a small cabin near Walden Pond on the outskirts of Concord, Massachusetts, in the 1840s. Among other things, this text emphasizes the beauty of woods that surrounded Walden Pond and the value of living a simple, solitary life, close to nature.

In the late nineteenth and early twentieth centuries, partly in response to the Transcendentalists, literary Naturalists, like Stephen Crane (1871–1900), Jack London (1876–1916), and Theodore Dreiser (1871–1945), presented a different version of nature. They saw it as an immensely powerful force that is completely indifferent to humankind, summarized eloquently in one of Crane's poems:

A man said to the universe:
"Sir, I exist!"

"However," replied the universe,
"The fact has not created in me
A sense of obligation."[1]

Literary Naturalism became a complex (and often misunderstood) literary movement that went well beyond the idea that nature needs to be respected and preserved, which is what most people associate with the term "naturalism."

Literary Naturalism is nicely illustrated by *SpongeBob Squarepants*, particularly the episodes "Nature Pants," "Squidville," and "Jellyfish Hunter." Like the works of Crane, London, and Dreiser, *SpongeBob* offers a subtle critique of the Transcendentalists' representation of nature by teaching us that by becoming civilized, human beings (and the animated citizens of Bikini Bottom) have lost the animal instincts that allowed them to be a part of the natural world and co-exist comfortably within it, and we are fools to believe our technology gives us power over nature or that (as Crane's poem suggests) nature has any vested interest in our continued existence.

"Nature Pants" and Jellyfish Instinct

The *SpongeBob* episode "Nature Pants" finds SpongeBob surprisingly discontented with his (usually beloved) job at the Krusty Krab, which he describes as a "cold industrial life"; in fact, he's so distracted that he sets the restaurant on fire. It turns out that he has become obsessed with the idea of moving out to Jellyfish Fields and living with the jellyfish. This seems to be an obvious homage to Thoreau's *Walden*, accurate down to the fact

---

[1] "A Man Said to the Universe," *American Poems*,
<www.americanpoems.com/poets/stephencrane/11798>.

that his foray into the wilderness is safely on the fringes of civilization, just as Walden Pond was a short walk from Concord. However, whereas, at Walden, Thoreau was able to "live deep and suck all the marrow of life, to live so sturdily and Spartan-like as to put to rout all that was not life, to cut a broad swath and shave close, to drive life into a corner, and reduce it to its lowest terms,"[2] SpongeBob did not find his Jellyfish Fields experience quite so transcendent.

Seemingly following Thoreau's advice to live a simple life, prior to abandoning his pineapple home in Bikini Bottom, SpongeBob gives away all of his worldly possessions, including a can opener and a jar of mayonnaise, eventually even stripping off his signature square pants, while boldly declaring that he does not "need all this stuff to be happy." He joyously sprints out to Jellyfish Fields to begin his new life, only to find that the jellyfish have absolutely no interest in him. In fact, they seem mildly annoyed by his presence, and they sting him relentlessly when he tries to interact with them.

It doesn't take us long to realize SpongeBob is ill-equipped to survive in the wild. He has no source of food, causing him to choke down a handful of grass for dinner, and when the jellyfish chase him out of their hive, he is forced to find shelter in a cave, where he sleeps, shivering, on the cold ground and is attacked by poison sea urchins. Unlike the spiritual awakening promised by the Transcendentalists, poor SpongeBob finds only misery and despair in nature. He misses his home, his friends, and the material comforts of civilization.

Both London and Crane would quickly identify the key mistake that SpongeBob makes. As he leaves, clueless and pants-less, for Jellyfish Fields, SpongeBob declares

---

2 Henry David Thoreau, *Walden* (Everyman, 1995), p. 72.

that he will rely on his "jellyfish instincts" to survive. SpongeBob obviously has no such instincts. He's not a natural being, but a civilized one who has grown dependent on the trappings of the modern world to survive. London emphasizes the effects that this loss of instinct has had on humans in his classic story "To Build a Fire."

"To Build a Fire" tells the tale of a nameless narrator walking through the Yukon in a seventy-five-degrees-below-zero temperature. His only companion is a "native husky" described by London as "a proper wolf-dog."[3] The dog is clearly still a part of nature; London points out that it still has instinct (instinct which is telling it that it's too damn cold to be walking around outside). The man in the story has no such instinctive voice inside him, and he also has a large ego, causing him to think he can overcome anything with his grit and intelligence—that he is too big to fail, if you will. As you might expect, his inability to comprehend the gravity of his situation leads to his tragic demise. Ultimately, as the bitter cold that comes pouring down from outer space takes away the man's life, his dog howls under the stars, reminding us of its animalistic nature, before allowing its instinct to guide it back to safety.

The message here is clear: humankind has lost its connection to nature—we are outside it now—and this puts us at the mercy of nature's mighty power at times. Another famous literary example of this is Stephen Crane's story "The Open Boat," which tells the tale of four shipwrecked men being tossed around by colossal waves as they desperately try to bring their lifeboat to shore. The massive size and power of the ocean is emphasized throughout the story, causing the men to feel very small indeed. And, as

---

[3] Jack London, "To Build a Fire," in *Literature: An Introduction to Fiction, Poetry, and Drama*, (HarperCollins, 1995), p. 119.

London does with the dog, Crane uses a seagull to remind the men that animals who are still a part of nature don't struggle with it the same way the men are forced to.

The men grow furious with the bird as it tries to land on the captain's head, both because the bird shows no respect for the dignity of the injured captain and because they are jealous of its ability to glide over the waves with such ease. It is not threatened by the ocean as they are because it is part of the same natural system that the ocean is. Civilization has driven animalistic instinct out of these men (and this sponge), preventing them from "going back to nature" as we sometimes romanticize about.

Squidward: A Cephalopod of the Streets

However these Naturalist writers (and the writers of *SpongeBob Squarepants*) also teach us that this same sort of cold indifference to humanity that the universe seems to have also exists in industrialized society as well. Both Crane's 1893 novella *Maggie: A Girl of the Streets* and Theodore Dreiser's 1900 novel *Sister Carrie* show us that the city can be just as difficult to navigate as the Yukon or the ocean or Jellyfish Fields. In both stories, young innocent girls are cast adrift in large cities. Although both young women interact with a variety of people, they find little true human compassion. Both become estranged from their families, and both end up crushed by their experiences (Maggie is literally killed and Carrie is spiritually empty in the end). It's suggested in both stories that, as Crane's poem says of the universe, the city seems to have no "sense of obligation" when it comes to the well-being of these poor girls.

A similar cold and indifferent urban community is seen in the *SpongeBob* episode "Squidville." In this episode,

SpongeBob's neighbor, Squidward Tentacles, grows tired of SpongeBob and Patrick always trying to befriend him, so he moves to the gated community of Tentacle Acres. Here he finds row upon row of identical houses, filled with fellow octopuses who not only look like him but who act exactly like him, showing him the kind of rudeness he had previously shown to SpongeBob and Patrick. Squidward is briefly happy in Tentacle Acres, but it is a bland and highly industrialized existence (they eat "canned bread," for heaven's sake).

Squidward is kept busy doing countless activities that he enjoys—modern dance, playing the clarinet, and so forth—but he's doing these activities next to other people, not really with them. These other octopuses are not his friends. They don't talk to him, other than to insult him or complain about his behavior, and they don't appear to care one way or the other whether he is there or not. This is sharply contrasted by SpongeBob and Patrick, who miss their neighbor terribly and go to Tentacle Acres with a cake to apologize to Squidward for bothering him. There are a few genuine human interactions in *Maggie: A Girl of the Streets* and *Sister Carrie* as well, but ultimately they are overwhelmed by the cold indifference of the city. Still, the message is clear: human beings (and civilized animated sea creatures) can, and need to, help each other out if they wish to not only survive but live a happy life.

This, it turns out, is the silver lining in what many readers see as the dark cloud of literary Naturalism: we can survive the indifference of nature if we stick together. In "To Build a Fire" the man had been previously warned by an old-timer "that no man must travel alone in the Klondike after fifty below." The story makes it clear that if he had a companion with him to help him build a fire after his feet got wet and his fingers went numb he probably would have survived. Likewise, in "The Open Boat," as much as the men's backs ached from rowing and as much as they feared drowning, there was something special about the fact that they were helping each other through the ordeal: "There was this comradeship, that the correspondent, for instance, who had been taught to be cynical of men, knew at the time was the best experience of his life." So although the literary naturalists sometimes frighten us with a cold, indifferent universe, they also celebrate the spirit of working together. Civilization may have driven natural instinct from us, but it has given us a powerful replacement: each other.

This is where SpongeBob excels. He loves pretty much everyone and he lives to help others, almost to a ridiculous extent, much to the annoyance of his next-door neighbor, Squidward. What Squidward fails to realize, however, is that this social interaction is a necessary component of a happy life. His hatred of his neighbors drives him to Squidville, but he ultimately misses the playful exchanges with SpongeBob and even reverts to SpongeBob-like silliness with a leaf blower to break up the boredom (which is what causes his uptight tentacled neighbors to ultimately turn on him and run him out of town).

However, naturalism also reminds us that even working together we are still far, far less powerful than nature. It is worth noting that despite their spirited teamwork, one of Crane's shipwrecked characters—the oiler, the one assumed to be the strongest—is drowned. Naturalist writers also remind us that when we abuse or try to exploit nature, it often leads to our own demise. For instance, the man in "To Build a Fire" is scouting for new fields of timber that could be taken out in the spring before he is stopped by the bitter cold. A similar warning against the attempted exploitation of nature is seen in the SpongeBob episode "Jellyfish Hunter."

It's Not Nice to Fool (with)
Mother Nature

"Jellyfish Hunter" opens with a narrative voiceover describing Jellyfish Fields as an "unpaved world of natural order," and we watch SpongeBob running through the green fields, catching jellyfish, quickly releasing them after gently tickling them with a feather to extract a bit of jelly. SpongeBob quickly spies a large, blue jellyfish (which he calls "No Name") that he has been unable to catch, and he begins chasing after it. However, there is no sense of anger or vengeance in the pursuit, just healthy respect, even when No Name eludes him once again.

Later, at the Krusty Krab, SpongeBob is taking his five-minute lunch break of a Krabby Patty topped with some of the jellyfish jelly he had gathered, when another customer asks for a taste and quickly declares it (in song) to be the greatest food he's ever eaten. Not surprisingly, Mr. Krabs see a huge profit to be made here, so he sends SpongeBob out to catch jellyfish (though Krabs mistakenly calls them "moneyfish") so they can extract the jelly. SpongeBob is conflicted because he loves jellyfishing but doesn't want to see the fish harmed. After Krabs ironically reminds him that there is "a whole ecosystem of hungry, paying customers" that they need to care for, SpongeBob agrees to catch some jellyfish for Mr. Krabs, on the condition that Krabs keeps them comfortable. At Krabs' incessant urging, SpongeBob has soon captured all of the jellyfish in Jellyfish Field except No Name.

No Name then follows SpongeBob to his home, symbolically cuts the power line to his house, and traps SpongeBob in a jar. He carries SpongeBob to the jellyfish processing factory that Krabs has secretly built (quoth SpongeBob: "Ew, what smells like big business?"). Here, the jellyfish are cruelly squeezed by a series of robots to extract the jelly. A horrified SpongeBob confronts Mr. Krabs, reminding him that "jellyfish need wide open space and fresh air."

Technology betrays Mr. Krabs as he accidentally frees the jellyfish by saying the word that opens the voice-activated door of his jellyfish tank. The jellyfish escape, but deliver a violent collective sting to Mr. Krabs before swimming off. SpongeBob thanks No Name, giving him the new name of "Friend," and promises to only use his net for "pure sport" in the future. No Name appears to forgive him, but he stings SpongeBob as they shake hands to seal the deal.

Once again, we're reminded that nature is stronger than humanity in the end, but those individuals with a healthy respect for nature can work with it, though at their own risk (which should not be underestimated). SpongeBob's tickling of a few jellyfish for an occasional snack seems innocent enough, but he easily becomes blinded by the excitement of catching "more, more, more" jellyfish and nearly wipes them out completely. This may make it seem as if civilized beings are stronger than nature, and certainly, as we have seen in real-life examples like the dodo bird, it is possible to hunt an animal to extinction, but that is a small part of a much larger picture. On the micro-level, humanity can control or exploit nature, sometimes to great human benefit, whether it be building homes out of timber or making a more delicious Krabby Patty. But nature always has an aspect we cannot control: bitter cold, a hurricane, a drought . . . or a big, blue jellyfish that knows how to use a wire cutters (admittedly that last one is pretty rare).

Friends—Don't Leave Home without 'Em

So where does this leave SpongeBob and Transcendentalism? Perhaps the most important lesson that SpongeBob and his fellow literary Naturalists teach the Transcendentalists is that they over-emphasize the benefits of a solitary life. Although Thoreau actually had frequent visitors at his cabin at Walden Pond, his book is filled with remarks like "I have a great deal of company in my house; especially in the morning, when nobody calls" (*Walden*, p. 103), which glorify solitude. In "Nature Pants" SpongeBob makes the out-of-character mistake of abandoning his friends when he goes to live with the jellyfish (which infuriates Patrick and frustrates Sandy), but when he finally gives up on his ill-conceived plan and returns home to his pineapple, his friends welcome him back with a surprise party and a group hug. Civilized beings (especially those with no jellyfish instincts to rely on—which is pretty much all of us, I suppose) need friends, and as No Name's final shock of SpongeBob reminds us, we cannot truly find friends in nature. Nature does have things to offer us, of course, but we must treat it with the utmost respect and expect no mercy from it. So go ahead and visit Jellyfish Fields, just bring a friend and don't throw away the keys to your pineapple.

PART III

You're Like a Steamed Vegetable, Only Smarter

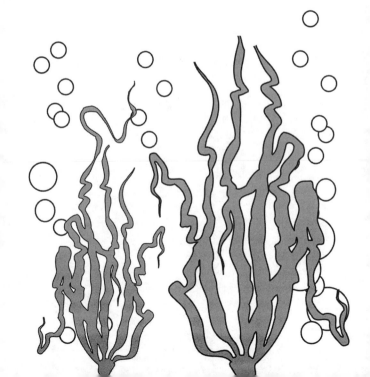

12
Does Anyone Have a Quarter?

The other night, I had a dream that I was watching an episode of *SpongeBob SquarePants*. The episode began like some episodes begin, with the image of an island and a palm. Cue the French Narrator whose voice sounds like a cross between Jacques Cousteau and the Monty Python and the Holy Grail character with the "ridiculous French accent":

> "AH, DREAMS. SO fascinating. SO wonderful. Here, we see Bikini Bottom, sleeping and dreaming in a peaceful slumber; home to one of my favorite creatures, SpongeBob SquarePants. Yes, of course he lives in a pineapple."

But wait, the narrator is suddenly interrupted by a more authentic French voice, the voice of philosopher René Descartes (1596–1650 C.E.) who suddenly casts doubt and skepticism into this vision of peaceful dreaming with his philosophical dream argument:

> "AH DREAMS. SO fascinating. SO doubtful. Here we see Bikini Bottom whose inhabitants believe they are sleeping in a peaceful slumber, but who cannot find definite signs to distinguish being awake from being asleep."

What brings the man known as "The Father of Modern Philosophy" here to interrupt the peaceful slumber of

Bikini Bottom in order to ask his enduring philosophical question, "Am I awake or asleep?" Why has the philosopher best known for his proposition "I think therefore I am" appeared to present his arguments from the "First Meditation" of *Meditations on First Philosophy* in 1641?

The episode "Sleepy Time" is a surrealistic romp through Bikini Bottom's dreamland that explores the questions of dreams and reality. During the DVD commentary for this episode, SpongeBob himself asks, "who's to say where reality leaves off and our dreams begin?" This question of where reality and dreams intersect or whether they are even distinguishable has been an ongoing philosophical argument, explored by Plato (428–348 B.C.E.), Aristotle (382–322 B.C.E.), Descartes and many others. In this episode, SpongeBob explores the dreams of his Bikini Bottom neighbors, which in turn allows us to explore the philosophical concepts of skepticism and dreaming.

Sleepy Time

SpongeBob is getting ready for bed. After warning his pet snail Gary to "watch his wandering eye" SpongeBob closes his eyes and a dream cloud appears. The dream is surreal and fantastic, with SpongeBob appearing in pieces, putting himself together and then driving a hotrod alongside a road decorated with larger than life pieces of a Krabby Patty. Anyone coming late to this episode would realize that it was truly a dream sequence because fans of the show know that SpongeBob does not have a driver's license. In fact, his on-going quest for a driver's license is a dominant theme throughout the series.

While zooming along, SpongeBob realizes that he doesn't have said driver's license. Shortly after, a driver's license appears, reminding us once again that this is a fantasy. As SpongeBob admires this long-sought-after object, he ignores the signs indicating the end of the road and promptly crashes. While soaring through the air, he meets Mrs. Puff, his beleaguered driving instructor. He shows off his driver's license only to have Mrs. Puff tear it up and let him know that he does not have one "even in your dreams Mr. SquarePants." With a tortured yell, SpongeBob continues to soar right out of his dream cloud.

A quick philosophical survey of the dream shows that it has elements of both fantasy (he has a driver's license) and reality (he will never get a driver's license). We also see that during this dream, SpongeBob demonstrates a form of consciousness in the realization that he is driving without a driver's license. This consciousness is an important element when exploring the philosophy of dreams.

Am I Still Dreaming?

When SpongeBob pops out of his dream, he finds himself as a smaller version of his larger self who is sleeping in the bed. When he sees himself, he asks the following philosophical questions: "Where am I? Is that me? Or is this me? Am I still dreaming?" The answers to these questions however do not appear to be of too much importance to him as he is immediately distracted from these ponderings by Gary's dream cloud.

The question "Am I dreaming?" has been asked and explored by many philosophers. Descartes in particular wrote about the problem of certainty and whether it is possible to tell the difference between dreaming and being awake. Descartes poses this question in his "First Meditation" of *Meditations on First Philosophy*.[1] He ponders the fact

---

[1] René Descartes, *Discourse on Method and Meditations on First Philosophy* (Hackett, 1980), pp. 57–60.

that he often dreams about events that occur in reality, such as sitting by the fire in his night attire which is what he is doing while writing these thoughts. Since he has had dreams where he is sitting by a warm fire in his pajamas writing great prose, how can he determine that he is not dreaming while he is in reality writing? The problem that he proposes is that there is no specific way or mark by which dreaming can be determined.

Many of Descartes's writings deal with skepticism and whether we should trust our own senses. These spill over into his thoughts on dreams as he suggests that we can never trust our own senses. If the senses can delude our dreams, senses can also delude our reality. The questions that Descartes raises about dreams are often presented as the Cartesian dream argument or dream problem, which searches for any philosophical proof that at any given moment one is not currently dreaming. Solutions to this problem have been proposed, argued, and refuted by philosophers since the problem was first put forward by Descartes.

Philosopher Norman Malcolm (1911–1990), in his book *Dreaming* (1959), deals with this dilemma by asserting that it is actually impossible to ask "Am I dreaming?" while in a dream because asking this question requires a consciousness that does not exist when one is asleep. The absence or presence of this consciousness during one's sleep is a contentious issue in philosophical discussions on dreams. SpongeBob's supposed consciousness of not having a driver's license, his out-of-body experience and questioning as to who he is and whether he is sleeping contradicts Malcolm's assertions about dreams.

Both Malcolm's and Descartes's assertions don't take into consideration the possibility of what's now called "lucid dreaming."[2] Lucid dreaming occurs when the dreamer is aware she's dreaming and continues to have the dream. The dreamer is able to determine that she is dreaming and to enjoy being able to experience things not normally experienced in real life. Malcolm would argue that this isn't possible as this requires a certain type of consciousness not possible in dreams. Descartes would argue that a dreamer can never actually determine that he is dreaming, thus cannot make the decision to jump out of the water and onto land without knowing whether he will frolic happily on the dry beach or dry up into a shriveled sponge. SpongeBob's ability to determine that he might be dreaming and his decision to continue the dream shows that he is perhaps experiencing such a lucid dream.

Watch Your Wandering Eye

While SpongeBob poses the questions that have occupied the minds of philosophy's great thinkers, he is not deeply concerned with the answers as he dream hops. SpongeBob warns Gary to "watch his wandering eye" before going to bed and cautions him to keep his curiosity at bay. However, during this dream sequence, it is SpongeBob who cannot help but wander into the dreams of Bikini Bottom residents to satisfy his curiosity and quest for knowledge and wonder.

When SpongeBob enters Gary's dream, he's shocked to discover that Gary can talk. In fact, Gary possesses a humanoid form and speaks and reads. Gary is in a large library which one could presume is filled with literature that includes the philosophical classics. On the DVD com-

---

[2] Jeff Warren, *The Head Trip* (Random House, 2007), pp. 112–155.

mentary, the creators ruminate that Gary actually looks like an "an intellectual or a philosopher." SpongeBob has asked the philosophical questions, but it appears that Gary is the one searching for the answers. When SpongeBob expresses shock that Gary can speak and read, Gary explains that one is "not tethered by earthly limitation" in dreams. SpongeBob asks what that means, thus questioning the nature of dreams, which is an important part in the dream argument discussion.

Gary attempts to explain to SpongeBob that dreams have been thought of as "windows to other realms." These other realms can be very different, or indistinguishable, from reality. Philosophers have not always agreed upon the true nature of dreams. Philosophers like Descartes believed that dreams are actual experiences within the sleeping state, while others, like Malcolm, don't view dreams as experiences but rather as illusions and ideas that are described during the waking state. Still other, earlier philosophers discussed dreams in their writings, with Plato speculating on the the possibility of the soul traveling in dreams, and Aristotle believing that people make judgments while dreaming.[3] Despite their differences, most philosophers would agree that dreams occur during sleep and can involve images or experiences that aren't possible when we're awake.[4]

Gary proceeds to quote Emily Dickinson attempting to describe the possibilities of dreams to SpongeBob. Failing again to get through to SpongeBob, Gary finds a limerick with which to educate his owner:

---

[3] David Gallop, *Aristotle on Sleep and Dreams* (Aris and Phillips, 1996), p. 12.

[4] A.J. Ayer "Professor Malcolm on Dreams," in Charles Dunlop, *Philosophical Essays on Dreaming* (Cornell University Press, 1977), pp. 127–28.

There once was a man from Peru,
Who dreamt he was eating his shoe,
He awoke with a fright, in the middle of the night,
To find that his dream had come true.

While Gary says condescendingly to SpongeBob that the limerick might be more his style, this limerick actually does address the philosophical question of dreaming versus reality as we see the intersection of dreams and reality in the events in the poem. SpongeBob thanks Gary for the information and exits the dream.

This dream provides an interesting insight into the character of Gary and his relationship with SpongeBob. Gary exists in reality as a sea snail that mainly eats, sleeps, and mews, but the dream-Gary is a thoughtful, philosophical, intelligent being. It's difficult for audience members to not view Gary differently after having been allowed to "invade the sanctity of his dreams" and learn of his intellectual pursuits. Going forward in the series, the audience knows that despite Gary's inability to speak, there is a lot going on under that shell, even if it is not always obvious that SpongeBob remembers this.

As SpongeBob leaves Gary's dream, he is warned by the mollusk to "watch his wandering eye," invoking SpongeBob's bedtime warning along with Plato's idea of the traveling soul during dreaming. Despite Gary's warning, SpongeBob follows his wandering eye into the dream cloud of his best friend, Patrick Star.

You Can Do Anything You Want

Much of Descartes's dream argument relies on the fact that dreams aren't always so different from reality. As mentioned previously, Descartes contends that it's possible to dream the mundane events such as sitting around in your

PJ's. Patrick's dream proves this contention and provides an excellent example of the type of dream Descartes invokes in discussing the difficulty of determining dream from reality.

When SpongeBob enters Patrick's dream cloud, he finds Patrick riding a twenty-five-cent kiddie ride. Patrick appears extremely content as SpongeBob asks him whether he realizes that this is a dream and that he can do anything he wants. Patrick acknowledges that he's aware that this is a dream, and indicates that he knows he can do anything he wants. SpongeBob is in disbelief that this is what Patrick would choose in his dream, and tries to illustrate the power of a dream by becoming as large as a skyscraper and multiplying himself. Patrick however does not appear to be dissuaded from continuing his simple dream. SpongeBob appears to be bored with Patrick's dream and announces that he's leaving. Patrick says goodbye just as the kiddie ride ends. He reaches into his pocket for another quarter to place in the ride, but drops it into a sewer grate. Upon announcing that that was his last quarter, he sits on the ride with a dull stare.

Even though he's aware that he is dreaming and that he could produce another quarter or even eliminate the need for more quarters, Patrick simply sits. The creators of the show comment that even Patrick's dreams are lazy. Once again, this dream gives the audience an insight into Patrick's own outlook on life. His dream temperament is similar to that of his usual real-life temperament; a happy, peaceful laziness. In fact, the scene so closely resembles reality that if one did not know that this was a dream sequence, there is nothing about Patrick's behavior, as Descartes would point out, to indicate that it was different from reality.

No More Messing with People's Dreams

SpongeBob continues to wander into the dreams of other Bikini Bottom residents. Each of these dreams provides insight and commentary on the characters and their relationship with SpongeBob. The "Sleepy Time" episode provides a nice set-up for the rest of the series. The audience has already been introduced to the main characters in previous episodes, but now we get to explore the dreams of the characters in relation to their life's philosophies.

Squidward Tentacles, the pessimistic foil to the optimistic SpongeBob is dreaming that he can actually play clarinet well as he performs a concert for King Neptune. Squidward is often attempting to achieve greatness through various artistic pursuits. It is not surprising that his dream would have him appearing as an undersea Mozart. His relationship with SpongeBob is so contentious that even the appearance of SpongeBob in his dream immediately invokes anger and frustration. These emotions are not unwarranted, as SpongeBob's actions usually lead to problems for Squidward. In reality, SpongeBob often attempts to counter these problems by helping Squidward with well-intentioned but misguided actions, usually making situations worse.

The dream episode parallels reality in that SpongeBob's actions (whispering Gary's limerick to King Neptune) meddle with Squidward's ability to perform and result in Squidward breaking his clarinet, much to the anger of King Neptune who threatens to cut off Squidward's head. SpongeBob's solution is to become a clarinet himself to replace the broken one. The audience reaction is positive and Squidward gets to keep his head. SpongeBob, however, becomes the main character in Squidward's dream as the fans are more interested in the instrument than the player, proving that even in his dreams Squidward cannot escape SpongeBob's interference with his life.

SpongeBob flees his adoring crowd and moves on to Sandy Cheeks's dream. Sandy, the adventure-seeking, adrenaline-loving squirrel from Texas, is para-surfing in her dream. As in real life, Sandy wants to share her love of adventure with SpongeBob and encourages him as they hurl dangerously towards a small target. Also as in real life, SpongeBob's lack of attention to detail proves to be a hindrance to the safety of both of them, as he produces a pair of shoes and a parakeet instead of a parachute. Sandy is so busy correcting SpongeBob that she falls into a truck full of clam manure before deploying her own parachute while SpongeBob lands on the target without a parachute. As with Squidward's dream, SpongeBob's presence in Sandy's dream has changed the course of the dream to be closer to the reality of day-to-day life.

Despite his claim that he will not "mess with people's dreams," SpongeBob can't help but wonder what his boss, Mr. Krabs is dreaming. When he arrives at Mr. Krabs's house, SpongeBob mistakenly enters the dream of Pearl, Mr. Krabs' daughter, who is having a tea party and invites SpongeBob to join her, but he declines. His brief time there only shows the audience that this dream is based on the reality that Pearl likes very girly things, including tea parties.

Mr. Krabs's dream is, as SpongeBob hopes, "more robust." In a nod to the reality that Mr. Krabs loves and covets money, his dream involves his quest for the great "Moby Dollar," an oversized dollar bill that he fishes from the sea. SpongeBob, as always, is ready and willing to assist his boss in any way possible, helping Mr. Krabs get Moby Dollar into the money net (a giant wallet containing Mr. Krabs's driver's license, which SpongeBob of course, admires). Again, as with previous dreams, reality sneaks in and SpongeBob unintentionally lets Moby Dollar get away. In this dream, as in reality, SpongeBob's supposed good intentions have prevented Mr. Krabs from achieving his constant goal of acquiring more money.

The final dream that SpongeBob visits is that of Plankton, the tiny scheming villain of Bikini Bottom. Plankton's ultimate goal is to steal a Krabby Patty in order to make his failed restaurant The Chum Bucket successful. His many failed attempts at procuring a Krabby Patty have often been thwarted by either his tiny size or SpongeBob's actions. In his dream, Plankton is a giant, zapping and stomping his way through Bikini Bottom. When he reaches the Krusty Krab, he stomps on it, destroying the restaurant—surprising, since normally he is attempting to get an actual Krabby Patty. Gary appears and is at great risk of being stomped on by Plankton, so naturally SpongeBob must rescue him. As Plankton is about to destroy Gary, SpongeBob turns himself into a pin, deflating Plankton to his usual small size. The tiny Plankton is promptly stepped on by a Bikini Bottom resident, thus ending Plankton's dream turned nightmare.

Stay Out of Our Dreams!

SpongeBob finally decides to return to his own dream and climbs back into his dream cloud. In his dream cloud is an image of his bed and he hops back in and climbs into the sheets. At this instant, the image in the dream cloud is the exact same image as in reality. His dream is perfectly mimicking reality with both dreamtime and real-life SpongeBob slumbering away.

Suddenly, the dream SpongeBob is surrounded by the angry faces of his friends yelling at him. He wakes up, much like the man from Gary's limerick, to find that indeed he is surrounded by the angry faces of his friends whose dreams he has visited. His friends implore him to stay out of their dreams because they get enough of him during the day and wish for a peaceful respite from his antics while they sleep.

It isn't clear in the scene whether SpongeBob even remembers having been in everyone's dreams. It's not he who relates his dream to his friends, but rather they relate the fact that he was in their dreams to him. Discussions among philosophers regarding dreams have not only surrounded the intersection of waking life and dreaming life but also focused on the acts of the retelling of the dream and remembering the dream. These are also important elements to exploring the nature of dreams.

Under normal dreaming circumstances, people are not held accountable for the actions and choices made during a dream. Even when relating a dream to a friend, generally that friend does not get angry for having been a part of the dream or for the choices made in the dream. In SpongeBob's case however, he's being held responsible for the actions and events that took place in the dreams of others, not even in his own dreams.

Do I Even Care if I'm Dreaming?

Returning to earlier discussions of Descartes's question of dreaming, we can ask if the events in the episode were dreams or reality. On the surface, it appears that the audience has just witnessed the interactions of the characters in dreamland as SpongeBob's wandering eye brought him through the dream clouds. However, during the final scene, Patrick appears and asks "Does anyone have a quarter?" This question connects the dream world to the current world and allows room for doubting the clear cut lines of dreams and reality.

Doubt is one of the major principles in Descartes's dream argument which questions our own senses and perceptions. In Descartes's "First Mediation," the narrator is so astonished by the realization that he could be dreaming that he becomes skeptical of both dreams and reality. This skepticism is at the heart of the dream problem and the many attempts to solve it. Doubt and skepticism however are not at the heart of SpongeBob. In fact, you could argue that SpongeBob is impervious to Descartes's skepticism as he never doubts or questions his senses throughout the episode; he just continues to follow his philosophical sense of wonder and adventure.

SpongeBob's solution to the dream argument is to ask the question, but not really care about the answer. He asks, "Am I dreaming?" but doesn't wait for the answer and most likely would not change his actions based on that answer. Instead, he continues on in his usual optimistic way regardless of whether he perceives it as dreams or reality.

This episode from my dream (or was it really a dream?) ends in Gary's dream. René Descartes has appeared, looking a little frustrated and harried. He has just encountered SpongeBob and attempted to argue the finer points of dream philosophy. However, as Descartes laments to Gary, SpongeBob did not seem to even understand what it is to doubt or be skeptical. It is impossible for Descartes to understand how someone can seek truth and knowledge without skepticism. Descartes believes that it's necessary to find an answer to doubt in order to confirm knowledge. In other words, we must be sure of when we are and aren't dreaming in order to be sure of the reality of being awake. SpongeBob's ability to seek knowledge without doubt has left Descartes baffled. Gary is sympathetic to Descartes's plight, grabs a book from the library shelves, and tries to help explain SpongeBob within the context of philosophy through this limerick:

There once was a sponge from the sea,
Who asked, am I dreaming? Is that me?
Not waiting around
For the answer to be found
He continued his ways regardless of dream or reality.

13

The Ego and the Squid

ROBERT JACOB KINCAID

SpongeBob bursts through a metal wall after Squidward mentions his heroes, Mermaid Man and Barnacle Boy. He needs an autograph. He already has an autograph at home; in fact, he has a signed copy of Mermaid Man's autobiography, but he wants—no *needs*—another. He harasses the superheroes, and ends up with Mermaid Man's belt after it's dropped in the heated retreat to the Invisible Boatmobile. Although SpongeBob initially tries to return the belt, he soon realizes just what it is he holds: Mermaid Man's Secret Utility Belt.

"I could just hold on to it until after work," SpongeBob says, rationalizing his actions, despite knowing full well that he should return the belt to the aged hero. When Squidward finds SpongeBob using the belt's shrink-ray to serve mini Krabby Patties to the cockroaches in the restaurant, Squidward chastises SpongeBob for holding on to the belt. SpongeBob, confronted with the truth of the matter and the threat of Mermaid Man finding out, mashes the buttons on the belt, shrinking Squidward so small that he can fit in Sponge's hand. But the nagging doesn't stop.

SpongeBob decides to visit his other neighbor, Patrick Star, his name popping up when SpongeBob tries to think of someone with "years of life experience." When the starfish tries to convince him that to reverse the effects of the shrink-ray he needs to turn the "M" for "mini" around and make it "W" for "Wumbo" the belt shrinks Patrick, too.

All of this is from "Mermaid Man and Barnacle Boy IV," which painfully documents the behavior of SpongeBob SquarePants in all his neurosis and denial. Even though SpongeBob *knows* that it's wrong to keep Mermaid Man's belt, he attempts to *minimize* the situation. *Minimization* is what psychologists call it when a person admits something is wrong but denies the seriousness of their actions through a process of rationalization. In the process he shrinks his two friends, the other parts of the mind, the conscience (Squidward) and his basic, instinctual desires (Patrick).

A Trip through Brain Coral Fields

SpongeBob's self-denial isn't too far-fetched when compared to the behavior of humans when faced with an unpleasant reality. Freud classified this behavior as *denial,* a type of *defense mechanism.* Defense Mechanisms help the mind deal with reality, often by ignoring it. It seems that SpongeBob can't get through a single eleven-and-a-half minute segment of his life without deluding himself about something or other. In Freudian terms he represents the Ego, who tries to reconcile conflicts between the Id and the Super-Ego and "reality." SpongeBob wants the utility belt, but his conscience nags at him and tells him that keeping it is morally wrong. His efforts to rationalize his continued possession are natural to SpongeBob; he's trying to avoid the unpleasant facts of life and fulfill basic desires.

The relationship between the three parts of the psyche is often artistically depicted as a bisected iceberg.

What's above water is conscious, while everything below the surface is subconscious. The Id is completely submerged, but the Ego and Super-Ego are both about half-and-half. This diagram makes little sense in this chapter, as everything I'm going to talk about will be completely below sea level, but it does provide a nice framework for understanding how the mind is represented in our actions. The Id resides in our subconscious, emerging only in terms of its influence on our behavior, while the Ego, that which shows itself in our interactions with others, attempts to compromise between those unconscious desires and the more authoritatively moral power of the Super-Ego.

Freud made a lot of claims about the way the mind works. He gave psychology something very important to consider: that you might be able to talk someone into sanity without taking such drastic measures as lobotomies or trephening. Trephening is a practice where one person drills into another's skull, usually to release demons or evil spirits. I'll say a lot of things about symbolism in *SpongeBob SquarePants,* but I promise that SpongeBob did not get his holes from trephening.

Freud's ideas about the mind have largely been dismissed by modern psychologists. Even those who thought that his assumptions were more than half correct tended to refashion his theories. Carl Jung (1875–1961) and Erik Erikson (1902–1994), for example, de-emphasized the role of sexual influences on human behavior, which heavily played into Freudian psychoanalysis.

Today most psychologists examine things like neurotransmitters, synapses and all the other stuff that makes the brain, and therefor the mind, work. They've moved past mere thought experiments and started studying other animals (or in the case of this chapter, cartoon aquatic life) to make comparisons to ourselves so that we can better understand our own development and behavior.

Despite the movement away from Freudian psychology as an empirical understanding of the human brain, his ideas are still important both as thought experiments concerning morality and as milestones in understanding what it means to be human. His model of the self can be used by the psychologists in order to help their patient construct a model of their own minds and resolve their problems. He identified and explained a lot of otherwise inexplicable behaviors and dared to talk about things no one else would (one of the reasons he is often labeled a "pervert").

Among the most important things Freud attempted to explain were the relationships we have with ourselves, our inner conflicts, and how those conflicts are resolved. He named and categorized defense mechanisms, ways that we cope with a harsh world. He identified actions like the sort of basic denial and delusions SpongeBob undergoes when attempting to rationalize his keeping Mermaid Man's utility belt, and moved to fantasy, which is to make-believe in order to avoid reality (like including a penny, a potato chip and a used napkin as friends to escape the cruel reality in "I Had an Accident"). He discussed the defense mechanism *regression*, wherein we attempt to sink back to an earlier version of our self to find peace, and repression, when we attempt to not like something that we obviously enjoy (like the way SpongeBob tries to repress his enjoyment of childish things in "Grandma's Kisses."

The Inner Machinations of My Mind Are an Enigma

SpongeBob, Patrick, and Squidward all live on some nameless stretch of road that varies in distance from the rest of Bikini Bottom depending on the day. The rest of the world is kept at a distance, and no one seems to come to this part of town unless they're invited or are on some sort of errand (mailmen delivering trophies for example).

Of the three, Patrick Star lives the lowest, underneath his rock, hiding himself from cultivation and education. His head comes pre-equipped with a dunce-cap. He has no goals, no worries about his future, seeking satisfaction through the most basic manners. He is the "it," the Id. According to Freud, the Id is defined by the "pleasure principle" in that it causes human beings to avoid suffering or pain and seek positive psychological and physiological states. Such is the reality of Patrick Star. Like the Id, he himself is unorganized, and seeks only to gratify his often sporadic and surprising cravings, and embraces a life of simple, rather hedonistic, pleasure.

On the other side of the spectrum, Squidward's home is strange and foreboding. It's furthest away from nature and it reflects Squidward's value of art. Squidward is stuck in his fast-food job despite his aspirations as a musician and artist because he cannot exist without SpongeBob, his repressor. He is the Super-Ego. He takes it upon himself to correct his neighbors, and teach them to behave in a manner that he feels is more sophisticated or proper, even though he is ever-unsuccessful.

Patrick's rock and Squidward's Easter Island Head are both very uninviting in comparison to SpongeBob's Pineapple house, a multi-cultural symbol for hospitality, housing the one of the three who most interacts with the outside world. SpongeBob's something of a man-child, responsible enough to live on his own, but not motivated enough to "succeed" as other people might. He has already reached his goal of employment at the Krusty Krab. He is the self, the Ego, the mediator. The Ego finds compromises between itself, the Id, the Super-ego, and the outside world. The Ego's job is to protect the mind as a whole, and so it fends off anything it fears might damage it: trauma, bad news, radical or anxiety-inducing information, and conflicts between the parts of the mind.

With these categories and representations in mind, lets walk through SpongeBob's decisions again. SpongeBob needs his umpteenth autograph why? Because he has idealized Mermaid Man as the super-heroic icon he *was*, not the senile person who walks around in his slippers and lives in a nursing home. He identifies with and wants to model his character after Mermaid Man. After he ends up with the belt he decides he will hold on to it for a little while, even though he knows he shouldn't. He makes excuses, so that he gets to eat his cake and have it, too, by "holding on to it for a while," all the while telling himself that he is going to give it back so that it isn't "stealing."

Squidward, the Super-Ego, looms over SpongeBob, laying the guilt on thick, so SpongeBob attempts to silence the other part of the mind by shrinking it. Then he shrinks the Id when he's talking to Patrick. He continues on this path of utilizing defense mechanisms till he hits rock bottom: delusion and denial. After enough pressure is applied he looks back to Mermaid Man for help. He shrinks everything in the town—including himself- to fit the new scale. Here he exhibits very altruistic behavior, followed by some humor; both top-tier defense mechanisms. But on some level SpongeBob, in fact, everyone, is still suppressing their own worries about the new size of the town—any worries are justified with the arrival of a regular-sized-and-towering-over-the-newly-shrunken-city Plankton.

What if SpongeBob hadn't fixed his mistakes? Perhaps he would have screamed and cried and gone into depression, wondering why the world was so cruel and unforgiving. SpongeBob is a crier, after all, famously making

Squidward a new sweater made entirely out of his own tears (though Squidward attempts to repress this perfectly normal behavior).

That's It! I'm Getting Off the Looney Express

Most of the show is based around SpongeBob, Patrick, and (often reluctantly) Squidward interacting with each other, but sometimes we get a glimpse of how the chemistry would work if the trio were changed to a duo, and on rare occasions, an episode about what would happen if only one of the three struck out on his own, essentially becoming the entire self. These episodes reveal more about each part of the mind and what we would be left with if any part of it were removed than we actually see in the episodes with all three primary cast members. There is no episode starring Patrick and Squidward without SpongeBob because without the Ego the Super-Ego and the Id can't interact. Without SpongeBob there Squidward and Patrick experience egolessness. Egolessness is an uncertainty if one exists separate from the world.

Egolessness is a sensation more than it is a feeling. Egolessness means not knowing if you're in control of your actions. It's that strangeness you feel when you've watched too much TV, played a video game for too long, or your car is veering off the road. Sometimes your instincts and reflexes take over and you keep singing "Having a wonderful time," even though your eyes are bulging and your adrenaline is pumping. Neither your mouth following the melody nor your arms steering the vehicle seem to be processes your mind is in charge of. After enough television you get the strange sensation of "Is this real? Am I thinking at all? Or is my body just going through motions?"

Squidward experiences something akin to Egolessness in "Squidville." After SpongeBob and Patrick annoy Squidward too much he yells at his neighbors. SpongeBob tries to defend his actions to the angry Super-Ego, but Patrick just drools. SpongeBob's protests are useless, though, since Squidward sees a commercial for a housing development called "Tentacle Acres," repeating verbatim what he just said about how much he hates his neighbors. After seeing the commercial he moves to a village of fellow octopi (yes, he's an octopus; they removed two legs because animation is easier with only six).

The octopi in Tentacle Acres all enjoy the same things. They all ride bikes, do interpretive dance (they all conform to dance in inexplicable choreographic unison), play the clarinet and like canned bread. Squidward montages through a few days and the widest smile ever seen on the cephalopod starts to sag into a deep frown. Squidward isn't sure what to do with himself. Squidward is surrounded with himself. He decides that he misses SpongeBob and Patrick and that without them life isn't interesting.

This also happens in "SB-129," where Squidward attempts to hide from SpongeBob and Patrick by locking himself in the freezer in the kitchen of the Krusty Krab. He is trapped and no one discovers him until Spongetron, a futuristic fry cook, unthaws him with a laser two thousand years in the future. After this jumping through time, Squidward eventually hits a form of purgatory in which nothing exists but him. Squidward is left alone. **Alone**. Alone. *Alone*. A͙l͙o͙n͙e͙. ALONE.

Yet Squidward hates being alone with himself even more than being around SpongeBob. The Super-Ego feeds off of the ego, and cannot survive without him, no matter how much it hates their connection or the ego's behavior.

The Super-Ego is constantly looking for ways to control the ego, and without Squidward around the balance shifts in Patrick's favor. When Squidward has left his neighbors to their own devices the two of them loose the ability to think in a forward manner. They indulge in the here and now and distract themselves, something that Squidward is painfully incapable of. SpongeBob and Patrick go to Robot Pirate Island, and though Squidward hears the sounds their imaginations make, he doesn't understand how they are made.

Patrick can't get by without SpongeBob, either. The friendship the two of them have built up defines them, and although they have their spats, they always return to being friends. Such a relationship seems straight out of Freud's writings about the Ego and the Id. "The Ego," Freud writes, "is not only the ally of the Id; it is also a submissive slave who courts the love of his master." SpongeBob and Patrick find a baby clam and decide to take it in. SpongeBob, despite being an asexual creature, becomes the "wife" to satisfy Patrick's whims, which are to wear a tie, carry a briefcase and to not do any work (Patrick is not at work, he's actually just next door watching TV). SpongeBob doesn't know that, however, and is happy to be the "wife" and make excuses on Patrick's behalf. For a little while. Eventually it's too much on SpongeBob to work the three or four extra sets of arms he's sprouted all day long and he snaps at Patrick.

When separated from SpongeBob, Patrick has difficulty even making it through the day. He wakes in the morning to find his alarm clock going off. But he doesn't even remember what the alarm is, his yesterdays never being spent on planning for today, not even enough to remember that he owns an alarm. He attempts to turn off the alarm clock through the method he assumes will require the least thought and effort: smashing it. An Ego like Patrick has a difficult time navigating the world with such impulsiveness and recklessness.

In the episode *Big Pink Loser* Patrick is jealous of SpongeBob's trophies; in essence, the Id wants the sort of reward one gets from long-term effort without putting in the long-term effort. Or maybe he just wants something shiny. When SpongeBob tells him that you have to earn your trophies Patrick agrees to work, assuming it would be no big deal. But Patrick Star has no drive, no work ethic, and absolutely no patience. SpongeBob has all of those things (even if SpongeBob's effort is all put into the Krusty Krab). SpongeBob eventually screams at Patrick, and Patrick gives up.

But without Patrick around the scales are tipped toward long-term thinking. SpongeBob and Squidward find themselves wandering the desert to deliver a pizza. Patrick would be against it, since it's boring and difficult, but he isn't there. Squid is against it because he hates everything to do with the Krusty Krab, a monument to unmet expectations and wasted talent. But SpongeBob and Squidward are both in it for the long haul, and without Patrick there to demand the end of their collective hunger, SpongeBob even resists the urge to eat the pizza, much to the detriment of his stomach.

What You Really Wanted Was Inside You All Along

Freud argued that there have been three major realizations that shook the human race's posturing as important:

1. **Realizing that the Earth isn't at the center of our solar system.**

2. **Realizing that we are just animals.**

3. **Realizing that we are *sick* animals.**

Freud included himself along with Nicolaus Copernicus and Charles Darwin, fancying himself as the final coffin nail in humanity's narcissism. Up until Freud the predominant action theory was agency, which is pretty much the theory that there is only Ego and that every action is evidence of the moral character of the Ego. Agency is the idea that humans (and possibly other intelligent creatures such as sponges and starfish) have the capacity to make choices and act on them and that the mind is not set in an inescapable causal chain.

Freud's theory, in contrast to agency, causes problems in the ethical branch of philosophy. Whereas Agency would lay blame on SpongeBob for holding onto Mermaid Man's utility belt, Freud and company have a harder time. Freud would have to ask if it's so wrong that the Ego was overpowered by the Id when he decided to keep the belt, or if the Ego was so wrong in shrinking the Super-Ego when it tried to voice complaints. So if SpongeBob acts only under duress from Squidward or Patrick can we really give him credit? If we do something good, but it's only because we don't want to feel guilty, should it be counted as a good thing, since the motivation behind it (to avoid discomfort) is amoral? Or if we do something bad, but because we are overpowered by our impulses, are we still to blame? Is it wrong or just animal weakness?

Imagine your mind minus the images of SpongeBob, Patrick, or Squidward. Imagine your actual mind. Imagine yourself in SpongeBob's position and imagine that the part of you that reminds you of Squidward functioning more like Patrick, or vice-versa. Without the guilty conscious pushing you to do this or without the primal urges pulling you to do that, do you think you would make the same decision?

In "Squilliam Returns," SpongeBob completely emp-
ties his mind so that he can fill it with information on how
to be a fancy waiter. Inside his mind hundreds of little
SpongeBobs are throwing files into shredders and dump-
sters. One of the SpongeBob-style workers says to his boss
inside SpongeBob's mind, "We don't even exist. We're just
a clever visual metaphor used to personify the abstract
concept of thought." Is the three-part theory the way the
mind works, or is it just a clever metaphor? If it is just a
metaphor, what does it say about us humans that we find
it so fitting? What does it say that we can keep information
from ourselves so thoroughly? What does it say about us
that our mind sometimes outnumbers itself? Freud would
have us believe that such inclinations demonstrate that we
are sick, and that perhaps it is time to pull up a couch and
lie down.

14
Sandy Cheeks, Scientist

WILSON GONZÁLEZ-ESPADA

Sandy's scientific presentation to introduce her latest invention has reunited many of Bikini Bottom's science enthusiasts in the Treedome. Once the misunderstanding with SpongeBob, Patrick, and Mr. Krabs was happily cleared up (SpongeBob was "Overbooked", Season 6) she continued her engaging discussion of her most recent invention, the Protogenerator 2000, a cloning machine (Note to self: get trademark rights for the suffix number "2000" after an invention's name). Of course, Sandy's conversation happened after the eleven-minute mark, so you did not have a chance of listening to Sandy describe the inner workings of the cloning machine and reflect about her sleepless hours pondering complex engineering and scientific questions. Trust me. It was awesome!

As I observed from the second row, right in front of that poor old fish who got beat up by a mob a few years ago (The Bully, Season 3), I wondered about the contradictions I saw all around me. There were a few instances where scientific inquiry was correctly portrayed. For example, the setting replicated the many scientific concurrent sessions I have attended over the years, conferences where the latest discoveries were discussed, evaluated, and challenged. It was uplifting to see a successful female scientist in a field where women have always been under-represented. And best of all, Sandy was presented without the caricature-like thoughts and behaviors of the garden variety cartoon scientist.

On the other hand, important aspects of science were ignored, very likely not to detract from the fun of the episode. Scientific experiments rarely use a single test subject; instead they use the largest possible sample size. Using a prototype device on a guy without at least earlier experiments with invertebrates or laboratory rats presents ethical challenges (Yes, I know, Spongebob is a sponge but you know what I mean). In fact, cloning still is a hot-button topic where the public and the scientific community are not necessarily on the same page. No wonder many people see conventional science in a stereotypical and often negative light.

From my second row chair my mind wondered for a moment, thinking that the public often perceive scientists as intelligent, but verbose and unable to communicate properly with the average person. As a consequence, most scientific endeavors, some of which were paid for by taxpayers, are simply not known or comprehended by them. I thought about the media, and how it perpetuates stereotypical views of science and scientists, which might lead to false assumptions about the nature of scientific inquiry.

Let's look at how science, scientists, and the philosophy of scientific inquiry are portrayed through Sandy Cheeks, one of SpongeBob SquarePants's closest friends. After our journey I am confident that you will see Sandy Cheeks as an admirable character who humanizes the thousands of scientists who dedicate their lives to describing and explaining the natural world.

Who Lives in a Treedome Under the Sea?

In the tradition of great Renaissance natural philosophers, and unlike most contemporary scientists, Sandy is knowledgeable in a number of scientific disciplines. Her talent as an engineer and inventor is most noticeable throughout the series as she has built, among other things, a moon rocket, a robotic nutcracker that also serves as a banana peeler, and a size-changing submarine to practice exploratory medicine. She is an experienced zoologist (in the episode "Wormy" she shows SpongeBob her animal collection, including ants, a turtle, a snake, a tarantula, ladybugs, a chameleon, an iguana, a frog, a cricket, birds, bees, and Wormy the caterpillar who wreaks havoc as he turns into a Monarch butterfly) and an accomplished moon-visiting astronaut, where she found no aliens whatsoever. I would not be surprised if she secretly is also an ethnographer, a social scientist who was sent to Bikini Bottom to describe and understand a society with unique cultural and social norms different from her own.

Sandy is not any cookie-cutter animated scientist! She is one of the latest in a series of cartoon scientists who have entertained children and adults worldwide for more than seven decades. How does Sandy Cheeks represents science in general and scientists in particular? To understand her contribution to how current and future generations will perceive science and scientists we need to first consider how scientists have historically been portrayed in television, movies, the Internet, and other media.

Children's Ideas about Science and Scientists

A number of prominent thinkers in the field of the philosophy of science have criticized the influence of popular culture's depiction of science as misleading individuals about the nature of science and scientific inquiry. Most notably, Richard Dawkins, a prominent ethologist and evolutionary biologist, has denounced the way in which

popular culture reinforces irrational belief in the supernatural over rational, scientific belief. That's what makes
the heroic qualities of Sandy Cheeks so important in helping to turn the tide of popular misunderstanding and apa-
thy towards the scientific enterprise.

The misperceptions about scientific inquiry abound.
For example, science teachers have relied on a very easy
test that is extremely powerful at identifying conceptions
and misconceptions of students in this area. The test is
called "Draw a Scientist" and simply asks students to get a
piece of paper and do their best drawing of a scientist.
The student work is carefully analyzed and the physical
characteristics of the drawn scientists and its surroundings
are noted.

After examining the drawings, most teachers will identify astonishing similarities. Almost all students, regardless
of gender, will draw a male scientist. Most students tend to
draw a scientist who is not a member of an under-represented racial or ethnic group. Many students include test
tubes, beakers, and other glassware, as well as lab coats,
goggles, and explosions. And yes, for some students scientists have made great discoveries, but a hair brush is not
one of them; crazy haired scientists are quite common.

When science teachers ask students if they would consider science as a career when they grow up, their
responses are also fascinatingly predictable. A typical student might say, "Thanks, but no thanks." Science is seen as
difficult and boring. Scientists are nerdy, goofy, and not
popular at all. They have few friends, show little emotion,
and speak with affectation and pomposity. Unless children
in America have a family member or a close friend who is
a scientist, their perception of what science is and what scientists do is shaped largely by the media. Kids have seen
hundreds of cartoons with evil scientists, or have watched
movies where science is used in a negative way, or have

played videogames where the scientist is rarely the good guy interested in understanding the natural world and its intricacies. As adults, they remain in relative ignorance about science and scientists, and maintain naive and unrealistic ideas about them. But, fortunately, Sandy Cheeks is in many ways a different kind of scientist, imperfect but refreshingly un-evil, un-crazy, and un-nerdy.

Sandy Cheeks as a Role Model

The first thing that I really like about Sandy is that she is a female scientist! That scientists can be female is not an obvious fact for a number of viewers. Breaking the gender barrier is something that has been an arduous and sometimes painful process in contemporary science. Consider the fact that in the United States fifty-one percent of all habitants are female and that there is no difference in intelligence and brain capabilities between males and females.

According to the report "A National Analysis of Minorities in Science and Engineering Faculties at Research Universities," social and cultural factors have contributed to female scientists being only 8.4 percent of mechanical engineers, 12.3 percent of electrical engineers, 14.3 percent of physicists, 21.2 percent of computer scientists, 22.7 percent of astronomers, and 23.7 percent of all chemical engineers. Other science areas where female scientists are slightly more abundant are mathematics (28.7 percent), earth sciences (31.8 percent), chemistry (32.4 percent) and biological sciences (46.3 percent). If you still don't believe that female scientists are scarce, try to think of the name of a female scientist who is not Marie Curie or Jane Goodall. No fair checking Wikipedia, either!

Sandy Cheeks is not only a female scientist, but a socially popular member of the Bikini Bottom community.

For example, in the Season 1 episode "Texas," SpongeBob, Patrick, and many other friends actively ask a homesick Sandy to stay living in their town instead of traveling back to her beloved state. Other show episodes present Sandy hanging out with friends, with the bodybuilder crowd at Goo Lagoon, and attending the Salty Spittoon. This is a welcomed departure from the often socially-awkward depictions of stereotypical scientists.

Have you noticed that most of the episodes where Sandy shows up are not science related? Even though this can easily be explained by the fact that the primary function of SpongeBob SquarePants is to entertain (otherwise you would watch it on PBS!), this is great news for those who might believe that scientists are extremely busy all the time, and eternally locked in a secret, inscrutable laboratory. Sandy has a life! Sandy has free time! If I would have to guess two of Sandy's favorite foreign phrases, those would surely be *joie de vivre* (Joy of living, a cheerful enjoyment of life) and *carpe diem* (Seize the day, live the moment to the fullest).

For Sandy, being a scientist is an exciting and fascinating career, a career she is proud of, but is a job nonetheless. She uses her free time enjoying a good conversation with SpongeBob, practicing sports like lasso, boxing, Frisbee, sand surfing, anchor tossing, extreme jacks, "kara-tay," riding bike in the park (the Industrial Park, that is), playing games like "find the hay in the needle stack," watching movies about Texas outlaws, reading a "Nuts" book, or protecting SpongeBob from condo scam offers. Sandy is not thinking about science 24/7 and neither are most colleagues in the scientific community. Real scientists plant gardens, walk on the beach, enjoy hiking, or play checkers. A highly recommended resource for those who would like to corroborate that scientists have "normal" lives after they punch out from work is "The Secret Life of Scientists and Engineers."[1]

And what about the misconception that most scientists work in isolated laboratories? Sandy Cheeks challenges this incorrect idea by living and working in a transparent tree-dome. SpongeBob and Patrick have visited Sandy's house on many occasions and it's not even locked! Sandy clearly recognizes that one of the basic principles of science is that it must be subjected to public scrutiny and peer review. Her open and non-secretive work environment is an accurate representation of how contemporary scientists share their life and scientific discoveries through publications, public lectures, and professional conferences.

If you think that scientists tend to be emotionally cold and calculating, like Mr. Spock from *Star Trek*, Sandy Cheeks will turn your frown upside down. Science is a human endeavor and humans are intrinsically emotional. Think about the times Sandy cares about SpongeBob and takes him to the doctor for a "suds" treatment, or organizes a multi-day search expedition for his missing friend (who is in fact hiding under a rock to avoid playing with the pre-hibernating squirrel), or tries to convince SpongeBob to return to society after abandoning it in favor of the simple and nude life of Jellyfish Fields. Unlike most cartoon evil scientists, Sandy shows compassion and a deep sense of friendship and commitment. She shows her humanity (It's really her "squirrelanity" but you know what I mean).

One thing that's especially charming about Sandy is her everyday, simple language when she communicates with her friends. Many stereotypical scientists are portrayed

---

[1] This is a web-exclusive interview series from NOVA, the acclaimed TV science series, available at <www.pbs.org/wgbh/nova/secretlife>.

as longwinded users and abusers of an arcane and compli-
cated language that shows off their mastery of the subject
while turning off all but the most science-oriented audience. Only a few eminent scientists, such as the late Carl
Sagan, Bill Nye, and Neil deGrasse Tyson, have increased
scientific literacy and public awareness of science with their
mesmerizing ability to summarize complex science issues in
a pristine language that is embraced by the average person.
In the episode "Chimps Ahoy" you can easily contrast
Sandy's colloquial style and those of her direct supervisors
from Treedome Enterprises Limited. When have you used
words such as ascertain, benefited, contraption, imperti-
nent, commence, or establishment, like the chimp scientists use? Who would call nose-picking "nostril evacuation"?

In one episode Sandy plans to leave Bikini Bottom
because she's unable to come up with an invention before
a deadline. In this case, Sandy appropriately shares the frustrations many scientist feel during the process of invention
and discovery. Science is intrinsically time consuming and
technically demanding, with trial and error and unex-
pected results being constant companions among scientists
in many disciplines. Scientists may take years to isolate a
protein, identify the function of a gene or enzyme, accurately describe a supernova remnant, or reconstruct a fossil.

As we can see, Sandy Cheeks is a radical departure from
the male, socially inadequate, workaholic, emotionless, secretive and verbose scientist that is imprinted in the public's collective mind based on fictionalized media venues. She is
definitely more in line with the real scientist next door and
contributes positively to the public perception of scientists.

What about the Science?

If Sandy Cheeks clearly presents a genuine portrayal of a
dedicated and down-to-Earth scientist, the show's percep-

tion of science itself is significantly less clear. There are instances when Sandy's behavior is consistent with basic tenets of the nature of science. In others, she is clearly not thinking like a scientist. For example, as far as I know, Sandy has never used Karl Popper's idea of falsifiability. In the philosophy of science, falsifiability assumes that any scientific question can be theoretically proved wrong. In other words, a claim that cannot be proved right or wrong is, by definition, an unscientific claim.

We can illustrate the idea of falsifiability with an example. SpongeBob believes that Squidward is his true friend by only considering confirming evidence, the few instances where Squidward has shown affection for him, and ignoring behaviors inconsistent with his belief. SpongeBob has collected only evidence that support his belief, a behavior that is not truly scientific. We can look at this scenario from a scientific viewpoint. SpongeBob could ask himself "Am I wrong in thinking of Squidward as a true friend?" SpongeBob could then try to find evidence that he is wrong about his claim of friendship. If SpongeBob can find just one counter example that he is wrong, then he can accurately conclude that Squidward is not really a true friend. As we know, given the personal dynamics of these two characters, finding such counter examples is not hard at all.

In the case of pseudoscience, the show offers a mixed bag. Pseudoscience is defined as an area of knowledge, belief, or process that is deceivingly presented as scientific when in reality there is no solid evidence or controlled experimental support for its claims. Of those pseudoscientific topics like extrasensory perception, aliens, ghosts, psychics, crystal healing, and astrology (not to be confused with astronomy, a legitimate science), aliens, and ghosts have been addressed in the program.

Sandy is clearly and correctly dismissive of alien life, at least on the Moon's surface. However, in an episode where SpongeBob and Patrick used invisible spray paint to pretend they were ghosts, Sandy ended up being truly scared. A rational scientist would ask him- or herself what was the simplest and most likely explanation, a prank or the theologically challenging notion of real ghosts? This line of reasoning is known as Isaac Newton's principle of parsimony: We are to admit no more causes of natural things than those that are both true and sufficient to explain a phenomenon.

Even though the viewers should not expect scientific realism from Sandy Cheeks's appearance in the series, incorrect representations of the nature of science and scientific inquiry might still be remembered by viewers, forming part of their mental science constructs. For example, philosophers of science distinguish between science as the knowledge gathered and processes used to systematically examine the natural world, and mathematics as the study of numerical patterns and relationships. They recognize that even though mathematics is a useful and commonplace language in science, it is not science itself. When Sandy shows SpongeBob a clip pad with the function and says "See this? This is science" she is incorrectly equating these important yet distinct subjects.

Philosophers of science have a clear definition of an experiment. In an experiment, you want to establish whether there is or is not a relationship between two things, usually called variables. The idea is that you alter or manipulate one of those variables (the independent variable) and you measure any effect on a second variable (the dependent variable) while keeping constant or invariable most of the other factors that might unduly influence the effect you want to see. In the show, Sandy incorrectly describes her inventions as experiments when in reality they are more like experimental equipment or engineering gadgets.

The episode "Chimps Ahoy" introduces the audience to two misconceptions about how most scientific research is funded in the United States. While it is correct that funding from private sources or public institutions like the National Science Foundation or the National Institutes of Health is contingent upon obtaining valuable information and results, the fact that Sandy will lose her funding if she is unable to come up with an invention within a few hours is an exaggeration. Real grant-funded scientists are required to provide frequent progress reports and will not lose funding even if the main experiment fails to show conclusive results. The principal way for scientists to fulminantly lose funding is if scandalous scientific misconduct occurs. Also, at the end of the episode Sandy is offered a twenty-year contract to continue her scientific activities. Real-life grants are funded for a shorter time period, usually three to five years. Scientists can re-apply for grants after that time period ends, usually with a different and improved version of the research study.

The Future of Sandy Cheeks

Sandy Cheeks is a very interesting character but her air-time seems to have diminished over the seasons. And of the times that she is a principal character in an episode, her science expertise is consistently underutilized. In my opinion, the show *SpongeBob SquarePants* has the challenge of preserving Sandy as a scientific role model for an ever-increasing audience while occasionally trying to integrate storylines that can be funny and sciency at the same time.

A perfect example of such science-related stories, even though Sandy did not have a protagonist role, was the Season 7 episode "SpongeBob's Last Stand." In this episode the construction of a highway that passes through Jellyfish Fields and Bikini Bottom leaves the scars of air and water pollution in a degraded and unhealthy environment. The episode ended with the removal of the highway and the return of the Jellyfish to lush grassland.

In reality, the environmental impact of highways is more pronounced and less likely to revert short-term and it can be a topic of discussion after watching "SpongeBob's Last Stand." Negative effects of highways and roads on the environment include noise pollution (which may prevent some species from communicating); the introduction of carbon monoxide and volatile organic compounds into the air; soil pollution with break and tire dust, as well as other particulates; and water pollution with gasoline, motor oil and de-icing chemicals. By fragmenting a habitat into sections divided by roads, animal mortality is more likely as they try to cross to the other side. Each habitat fragment will have less biodiversity, promoting inbreeding and a poorer genetic pool.

Similar messages about environmentalism and biodiversity can be seen in episodes like "Jellyfish Hunter" where Mr. Krabs uses SpongeBob's love of jelly fishing to ignore the interrelatedness of the biosphere and overexploit Jellyfish Fields for an irresistible Krabby Patty topping. Mr. Krabs's quest for economic gain at the risk of driving jellyfish to local extinction is antithetical to Aldo Leopold's widely accepted vision of environmental ethics, where conservation is defined as a way of life in which nature does well for its inhabitants, citizens do well by nature, and both end up better because of this symbiotic partnership.

Despite some inaccuracies in her depiction of scientific inquiry, the contribution of Sandy Cheeks to the portrayal of a more accurate version of a working scientist should not be underemphasized. Our friendly squirrel should set an example for more well-meaning and nice scientists in future cartoon series. Although the media's main objective is to entertain, its far-reaching nature provides a unique opportunity to introduce discrete aspects of science and social responsibility into story lines. The power of cartoons can be harnessed to increase the public's perception of science and scientist, the way Sandy Cheeks does, karate and all.

15
A Sponge's Insatiable Thirst for Knowledge

Robert S. Vuckovich

Something mysterious dwells at Bikini Bottom. In the episode, "The Secret Box," Patrick Star keeps something from his best friend, SpongeBob SquarePants, rousing a temptation that affects the good-natured sponge's desire to know. What's surprising about Patrick's secret box isn't its content. Instead, it relates to SpongeBob's interest in knowing what's in the box.

Historically, a person's reason or intellect determines how knowledge is acquired. From Plato's dialogue, *Theaetetus*, wonderment functions as the birth of philosophy. Plato (430–347 B.C.E.) considers that an intrigued mind will investigate all that it does not fully understand in order to discover the truth. Nothing beyond that account is discussed throughout the remainder of the dialogue. It's ironic that the dialogue ends without the particpants coming to know what knowledge truly is.

The dialogue between SpongeBob and Patrick seems less profound than anything Plato has produced, but the philosophical dilemma that develops between these friends about how to acquire the knowledge of a secret puts a sinister spin on Plato's notion of wonderment. The attention given to Patrick's secret box reveals how intense an individual's desire to know a secret can get.

It's only fair for us to wonder whether this philosophical investigation into the desire to know, using SpongeBob as the example, may expose a secret side to wonderment that possibly Plato didn't know about or want to know.

You Can't Handle the Truth

When Patrick initially sets off SpongeBob's interest to know what's hidden in his secret box, tensions develop between the friends as SpongeBob pesters Patrick to disclose what's inside. Patrick's constant reminders that there is an unknown truth, and that if SpongeBob had knowledge of this truth it would change his life, intensify the sponge's thirst for knowledge. By showcasing the secret, Patrick plays the dual role of both the secret's guardian and its promoter.

For SpongeBob, there's literally an opening to discover that which he is "to never find out" due to the guardian's inability to keep the secret a secret. Important to this slight breach is that Patrick tempts SpongeBob's desire to know, creating urgency in his truth-seeking inquiry. Bringing his secret box to light makes Patrick appear similar to a Socratic midwife. Perhaps instigation is Patrick's way of testing to see whether SpongeBob truly has a desire to know what is kept hidden from him.

The purpose of a secret eludes SpongeBob's understanding. He tells Patrick that "the best thing about a secret is secretly telling someone your secret. It's like secretly adding another secret to their secret collection of secrets." Indeed, SpongeBob simply wants the truth to be known, by having Patrick divulge it, which philosophically puts an end to the importance of wonderment as Plato suggests. Having Patrick reveal the secret suggests that SpongeBob makes no effort in discovering the truth for his own intellectual development.

Most of Plato's dialogues question and examine what people know. But knowledge is not restricted to the inquiry of things unknown; rather, an individual's character can develop through the acquisition of knowledge. Sometimes, though, when a particular truth is not readily apparent or discernable, an individual searches for the truth. It's then a matter of how knowledge is acquired and what one does with it that determines one's character.

SpongeBob's desire to know turns into desperation when he shares an abundance of his so-called personal secrets just to get Patrick to share his lone secret. This *quid pro quo* exchange doesn't interest Patrick, for he remains steadfast in keeping his secret from everyone, even Squidward's supposedly inanimate house. Calling SpongeBob "an open book" confirms the view that his friend has no appreciation for safeguarding secrets.

In another desperate act, SpongeBob deliberately snatches the box while Patrick is caught off guard, for he cannot resist knowing the secret and is compelled to resort to using covert methods. Never in Plato's talk of a budding philosopher do we hear him characterized as being sly in his pursuit of knowledge. So what is it about SpongeBob's desire to know Patrick's guarded secret that makes him less appealing not only as a philosopher, but as a decent person?

Curiosity Kills the Sponge

Two millennia after Plato, Thomas Hobbes (1588–1679 C.E.) offers an overview of human nature, which includes a detailed account of how the mind works. Reason, which many ancient philosophers esteemed, loses its pristine stature. Hobbes believes that knowing the truth is not fully possible due to each man's desire to declare that he alone claims to know the truth.[1] Without getting into details about how knowledge is formed, we should consider Hobbes's perspective on wonderment. Categorizing the desire to know as a "voluntary motion," much like other passionate desires, he calls curiosity "a lust of the mind" (pp. 44–45). This characterization suggests that an individual with a curious mind has a persistent appetite for knowledge. Unlike the good-natured Theaetetus, but identical to SpongeBob, an individual with that mindset can become overly preoccupied with wanting to know.

Unable to sleep that night, SpongeBob formulates a series of possibilities of what could be in Patrick's box. As SpongeBob's mind contemplates each possibility, his fascination escalates, transforming the secret, and even his friend, into something disturbing. Resistance is futile, for it is now imperative for SpongeBob to know. The manner in which Hobbes equates curiosity with other pleasure-seeking passions shows how compulsive an individual's mind can become, even for the sake of knowledge.

Lust accurately describes how SpongeBob's mind operates, because he devotes so much time wondering about the secret box. His fixation on it makes him want to know, or, better still, possess Patrick's secret. Curiosity possesses him so much that he intends to discover the secret without Patrick knowing. Selfishness of this kind constricts the learning process, because other forms of rational thought are ignored. SpongeBob fails to fully comprehend how his scheme to discover Patrick's secret will end their friendship, if Patrick should ever find out. It is a gamble SpongeBob, without consideration for the potential loss, is willing to take. But is risking his friendship for the sake of knowledge in SpongeBob's best interest?

---

[1] Thomas Hobbes, *Leviathan* (Broadview, 2002), pp. 34, 35.

Enthralled by his scheme, SpongeBob may never have wondered about it.

It's difficult to determine whether the desire to know is as good as Plato surmises when the individual is so focused on one particular thing. Philosophy is often called the love of truth, but what happens when that love for discovering the truth pervades an individual's thoughts? Is SpongeBob an example of a philosopher whose love of knowing has become obsessive, for he admits that uncovering the truth of Patrick's secret will be "the last thing" he must do? With that as his sole mission in life, it might be funny to see whether this episode would have lasted longer than just one episode, especially if Patrick's secret remained undiscovered by SpongeBob. Could SpongeBob's curiosity die out?

Hobbes maintains that curiosity lasts longer than other passions, even carnal passions, if and only if knowledge continues to develop within the individual (p. 45). But SpongeBob is dying to know one thing—that which only Patrick knows. Once he discovers Patrick's secret, he achieves fulfillment. Here knowledge kills curiosity. What's most profound about this point is that the acquisition of knowledge purges, or relieves the tensions in SpongeBob's perplexed mind. Wonderment is seen as personal torment. Ignorance, then, must seem like the worst form of agony anyone can experience. Perhaps the Socratic role of a midwife bringing knowledge to the fore is the therapeutic way of easing this suffering. Given Socrates's description, midwives "either bring on the pains of travail or allay them at their will, make a difficult labor easy, and at an early stage cause a miscarriage if they so decide" (*Theaetetus*, p. 854).

If this torment becomes intolerable for SpongeBob, he does himself a service by uncovering the mystery of Patrick's secret box, for he no longer frets over what he does not know. Yet, in his attempt to discover the truth, SpongeBob must overcome the dilemma of ending his torment without ending his friendship with Patrick. If his scheme succeeds, his torment ends, the friendship is preserved, and he has his own secret that Patrick does not know about. One must remember, though, that SpongeBob by his own admission is keen on disclosing secrets as opposed to keeping them. It's rather paradoxical for him to take pride in concocting a secret scheme.

Before SpongeBob begins his quest for this elusive secret, he seeks justification for this undertaking. A stumbling block gets in the way of his pursuit for the truth. When SpongeBob consults his pet snail for some positive feedback about his plan, Gary, acting as the voice of moral reason, objects to his master's secret objective. Obviously, SpongeBob has already spoiled his own secret by seeking support. Since SpongeBob lusts after Patrick's secret, he rejects his pet's objection as coming from someone who doesn't comprehend the value of another individual's desire to know.

What's in the Box?

Perhaps Patrick isn't guarding any secret. Given that "the inner machinations" of Patrick's mind are "an enigma," you might think that he's out to perplex everyone in Bikini Bottom with nothing. This possibility never crosses SpongeBob's mind, probably because he witnesses Patrick taking pleasure from what's inside. Additionally, Patrick goads SpongeBob about "the greatness of the secret box." These enticements are truly hard to resist, which likely make SpongeBob incapable of breaking free from his urge to know.

But is there any real danger in knowing a secret? This question is not suggesting that Patrick's box is comparable to the ancient myth surrounding Pandora's Box, whereby if that box is opened, all sorts of horrors would plague the world. None of Patrick's warnings indicate anything menacing. Instead, there are consequences if the secret is not preserved. SpongeBob has the opportunity to acquire knowledge of the secret or preserve the secret, which in turn preserves his friendship. Avoiding knowledge seems like the best option if and only if SpongeBob cares about the friendship.

In keeping with Plato's optimistic stance on knowledge, consider what is said in the dialogue, *Charmides*. Socrates's interlocutor, Critias, deduces that "if you discard knowledge, you will hardly find the crown of happiness in anything else."[2] Similar to the *Theaetetus*, Plato does not elaborate on what knowledge is in this philosophical discussion. Never does he seem to take knowledge off its regal pedestal. Important to SpongeBob's predicament is that knowledge of the secret would most assuredly bring him happiness. Yet the one condition for attaining this happiness is that Patrick isn't supposed to know about it. So SpongeBob's happiness can never be shared with his friend. Consider also how unhappy both friends will be if Patrick knows of SpongeBob's secret scheme.

The question relating to what's in the box is not the only question raised in the episode. During SpongeBob's fanatical musings, he questions Patrick's character. Suspecting him of being a jewel thief in one instance and a deranged maniac the next is how SpongeBob not only fuels his own desire to find out whether these groundless speculations are true, but also justifies his urge to investigate his friend's secret, because it seems peculiar that

---

[2] "Charmides," in *The Collected Dialogues of Plato* (Princeton University Press, 1989), p. 119.

Patrick would keep such a secret from him. Questioning the integrity of his friend makes his investigation all the more necessary to him, for there are additional truths worth discovering.

To wonder what's in the box pales in comparison to the thoughts that preoccupy SpongeBob's mind. The latter question is more philosophically intriguing and is worth a look-see. Though that question does little for the study of knowledge, it offers insight into morality.

The Purloined Peek into Epistemological Morals

Moral dilemmas typically don't accompany what Plato or Hobbes have in mind with their views on the development of knowledge. Throughout Plato's dialogue, *Republic*, the moral lesson is that no individual commits a wrong knowingly. When SpongeBob elaborates on his notion of secrets out in the open, and when he begins his secret mission to discover Patrick's secret, one wonders whether SpongeBob understands the moral repercussions of his epistemological venture. As mentioned, Gary acts as SpongeBob's conscience once the scheme is hatched, but is ineffective in restraining his master's insatiable desire to know. Evidently, SpongeBob lacks his own conscience at this stage. Otherwise, he wouldn't go through with his scheme.

There is no reflection on SpongeBob's part as he breaks into Patrick's home to sneak a peek inside the box. SpongeBob has cleverly formulated how the best possible scenario would work, so he can satisfy his epistemic lust and preserve his friendship with the hoodwinked Patrick. With an element of deceit key to his pursuit of knowledge, SpongeBob not only knows that he is doing his friend wrong, but he intends on doing so.

Unlike Gary, Cicero (106–43 B.C.E.) would harshly disapprove of both SpongeBob's intentions and subsequent actions on the grounds that "no greater curse in life can be found than knavery that wears the mask of wisdom."[3] Incidentally, SpongeBob wears a mask to conceal his identity, signifying a deliberate attempt to hide his deceitfulness as he sneaks into Patrick's home. Note that SpongeBob did assure Patrick that he respects his secret. No matter how ingenious his secretive plan is, he carelessly betrays his friend regardless of whether he discovers the secret. SpongeBob seems oblivious to how his actions could hurt his friend psychologically.

Although SpongeBob's objective is to acquire knowledge of "one great secret," his modus operandi is morally offensive. It is a selfish enterprise for SpongeBob to know without others knowing how he came to know. Both SpongeBob and Patrick prevent each other from knowing what the other is keeping secret. The major difference between SpongeBob's and Patrick's respective secrets is that SpongeBob and his actions are the secret, something a bit harder to conceal in a box. Expressed differently, keeping a secret is not the same as intentionally making something a secret. Besides, Patrick's secret, however guarded, is made a spectacle, whereas SpongeBob's secret is supposed to remain hidden as though the entire episode never actually happened.

SpongeBob SecretStealerPants knows this all too well, for his curious mind has formulated the scheme. He has committed a deceitful offence against a friend for the sake of dishonest gain, which in his mind is a quest for knowledge. Consider Cicero's characterization of a dishonest mind engrossed in such a pursuit: "For how few will be found who can refrain from wrong-doing, if assured of the

---

[3] Cicero, *de Officiis* (Harvard University Press, 2005), p. 343.

power to keep it an absolute secret and to run no risk of punishment." Yet there is no absolute assurance for SpongeBob, for he relies on cunning. Patrick discovers that his friend has underhandedly come into possession of the secret box and punishes the thief by terminating their friendship, even though the secret remains unknown to SpongeBob. Having SpongeBob's secret exposed inadvertently exposes him for who he truly is. One wonders whether SpongeBob realizes that his curiosity has killed this friendship.

There is an underlying dilemma to this story, namely, friends keep secrets from each other. Did Patrick's and SpongeBob's respective secrets contribute to ruining their friendship? If Patrick shared his secret, then SpongeBob wouldn't have gone to the trouble of secretly trying to peek into Patrick's secret box. This gesture would satisfy SpongeBob and ultimately end the secret. However, taking a peek is SpongeBob's way of taking the friendship for granted. Again, Patrick is quite open about having a secret, whereas SpongeBob cannot afford to reveal his. Connecting this point to Plato's notion of wonderment and Hobbes' account of curiosity, one cannot find fault with Patrick, because SpongeBob is consumed by a seemingly insatiable interest to know what his friend is keeping from him.

Valuing friendship the way SpongeBob does is alarming, in that he, as part of his scheme, uses deceit to preserve the friendship. SpongeBob cherishes his desire for the truth over his friend's wishes. Yet his friendship is not expendable. He does deserve some credit for not wanting to spoil his friendship with Patrick, despite the fact that the approach he undertakes, however secretive, undermines the friendship. Besides, if SpongeBob succeeds in knowing what the secret is, he must, in order to preserve their friendship, continually deceive Patrick into thinking that he doesn't know the truth hidden in the box.

Ignorance would be bliss just as long as SpongeBob no longer concerns himself with knowing Patrick's secret. It becomes a challenge for him to control his curiosity. An exercise of this type of resistance never presents itself in the episode.

Perhaps there is one thing that SpongeBob truly ought to know. When he wonders what's in the box, he should wonder about himself. Critias in the *Charmides* comes to realize "that self-knowledge is the very essence of temperance" (p. 110). This rational quality enables an individual to resist an assortment of personal pleasures, interests, and possibly curiosities. Given SpongeBob's desperate need to know, one can recognize how such a quality would keep him from looking into his friend's private domain because of his inherent lust. Self-knowledge may redirect SpongeBob's focus on things unknown to those which he already knows will make him happy, such as being "friends forever" with Patrick.

The most surprising thing about SpongeBob is that he doesn't learn lessons very well. He remains oblivious to keeping secrets, even when he comes close to losing his best friend. Shortly after Patrick allows him to look in the box, he leaves for home and announces that he has to tell Gary what he saw. Patrick's earlier characterization of his friend confirms the perspective about an open book's inability to stay closed.

Secret Revealed . . . I Wonder?

Given that the inner machinations of Patrick's mind are an enigma, most of us are surprised that he suddenly allows SpongeBob to look into the secret box. The revelation not only discloses what is inside, it also shows that SpongeBob's curiosity remains fervent, completely forgetting that his friendship has just about ended. If SpongeBob really had any misgivings about how he tried to undermine his friendship, he could have refrained from taking up Patrick's offer.

Plato does not believe every individual is philosophically inclined. Only mature-minded individuals are capable of grasping and knowing what is a mystery to them. SpongeBob has proved that he isn't one to pry into mysteries, especially when there are undesired consequences associated with them. He serves as an example of how a wondering mind shouldn't be so fixated. The fixation amplifies his inability to distinguish moral predicaments and their outcomes. Although his mind appears fully functional, its operations need to relax and follow better directions. Containing his desire to know may make SpongeBob more open-minded about how significant the secret box is to his friend. It is rather ironic that curiosity closes his mind to wanting to know one box-sized secret.

Mysteries like a secret box keep a curious mind active. Minds would likely become dull if there were no secrets to examine and hopefully expose. Then again, some secrets might be best left alone.

Were you curious to think that Patrick is guarding a secret that might harm his friend in some form if he were to find out? If so, this genuine concern would demonstrate that Patrick acts in his friend's best interest. Acquiring knowledge would then seem unwanted to SpongeBob if he knew Patrick cared about him so. Yet SpongeBob does not esteem friendship in the same dignified manner as Patrick does. With a friend guarding a secret, the temptation to know it must perplex SpongeBob so much that he will always remain curious about what Patrick is hiding. Watching him resort to such crafty measures to find out the truth, we viewers witness how misguided and insensitive an inflexible, undeveloped mind can be. Maybe

Patrick should take the initiative to preserve the friendship as well as the secret.

The likelihood that SpongeBob can contain his curiosity on his own is doubtful. So when Patrick hands the secret box over to his friend, it isn't surprising that SpongeBob exhibits no compunction when given the opportunity to "look inside." This response is expected according to Hobbes's conception of a lustful mind. Patrick sates his friend's fixated curiosity. The seemingly insatiable desire to know that torments SpongeBob from the beginning fizzles out once the secret box is open to him. This state of epistemic wonder is gratifyingly momentary. The problem here is that as SpongeBob's curiosity fades, his knowledge of the secret box's interior ceases to fascinate him. Patrick has shown that his friend's desire to know lacks the acuteness that Plato would find necessary for an individual to conduct a thorough philosophical investigation. SpongeBob in the end never considers that the secret box contains an additional secret.

It's no secret that SpongeBob is by Platonic standards no budding philosopher. Earlier, it was suggested that Patrick functions like a philosophical midwife. Although Patrick hands over the box, he guards the secret by testing how curious SpongeBob is. With the sole objective of peeking inside the secret box, SpongeBob prematurely aborts his thirst for the truth, because as Patrick informs him of something secret in the box, SpongeBob's epistemic expectations get disappointed at what he sees. He therefore gives up on his desire to know.

How unfair is it that Patrick still keeps a secret from SpongeBob? Yet guarding it is Patrick's way of safeguarding their friendship. As a philosophical midwife, Patrick acts as SpongeBob's guide, making certain that his friend's pursuit of knowledge is burden free. Cicero would articulate Patrick's obligation as such: "it is not the province of a friend . . . to have the same estimate of another that the other has of himself, but rather it is his duty to strive with all his might to arouse this friend's prostrate soul and lead it . . . into a better train of thought."[4] So when SpongeBob claims, after his first attempt at peeking inside the box, to respect Patrick's secret, Patrick ensures that his friend stays true to his words.

So is Patrick deceiving SpongeBob for not revealing the secret of the box?

Patrick has been rather open with his friend. Since it's SpongeBob who sets out to secretly discover his friend's secret, he unknowingly creates a new secret by not examining the secret box beyond his peeking inside. He looks, but does not search. His curiosity dies at the moment when he believes he knows the secret. No true knowledge has been gained and thus no secret is lost. This episode ends in a manner typical of most of Plato's dialogues, whereby the participants have arrived at their initial starting point, not knowing much. SpongeBob finds reassurance by returning home and knowing that Patrick remains his best friend despite his deceitful search for the truth. Thoroughly amused by this outcome, Patrick continues to guard the secret box by keeping SpongeBob's curiosity secretly boxed up.[5]

[4] Cicero, "de Amicitia," in *de Senectute, de Amicitia, de Divinatione* (Harvard University Press, 1992), p. 169.

[5] Most of the initial ideas for this paper arose out of a discussion I had on *SpongeBob SquarePants* and the episode, "The Secret Box," in Makati City, Philippines. I had to explain to the staff at BPO International why a middle-aged man takes an interest in a cartoon and elaborate on its moral significance. So I thank them, especially Shey, SpongeBob's number one fan in the Philippines, for participating and helping me develop the issues presented now in print.

Denizens of the Deep

GREG AHRENHOERSTER is an associate professor of English at the University of Wisconsin-Waukesha. He has published articles on the symbolism of sports in American literature and contributed a chapter to the book *Homer Simpson Goes to Washington: American Politics through Popular Culture* (2008). He has three children who have most of the episodes of SpongeBob committed to memory; sadly, the sixteen-year-old seems to have absorbed SpongeBob's driving skills, but the thirteen-year-old makes a mean Krabby Patty, and the nine-year-old has a great I-MAG-I-NA-TION.

KATIE ELSON ANDERSON is a Reference Librarian and Web Administrator at Paul Robeson Library, Rutgers University. Her publications include contributions to the *World History Encyclopedia* (ABC-CLIO, 2010), *Encyclopedia of Social Networking* (2011), *21st Century Anthropology: A Reference Handbook* (2010), *Teaching Gen M: A Handbook for Librarians and Educators* (2009) and *Scholarly Resources for Children and Childhood Studies* (2007). Ms. Anderson has co-edited the book *Stop Plagiarism: A Handbook for Librarians and Educators* (2010). She has presented work at both the regional and national Popular Culture Association conferences on the topic of "Storytelling in the Digital Age." Ms. Anderson drives a VW named "Patrick Car" and always drinks her tea with her pinky up.

ADAM BARKMAN is Assistant Professor of Philosophy at Redeemer University College. He is the author of *Through Common Things: Philosophical Reflections on Popular Culture* (2010) and *C.S. Lewis and Philosophy as a Way of Life* (2010) as well as the co-editor of *Manga and Philosophy: Fullmetal Metaphysician* (2010). He's extremely grateful to his two-year-old daughter, Heather, who showed the greatest interest in Daddy's "research" for his chapter in this book.

MICHAEL DODGE is a Boeing Fellow of Air and Space Law at McGill University. He has studied biology, law, and philosophy, where his interests are primarily in logic and the philosophy of science, and he is currently Chairman of the Philosophy and History of Science Division at the Mississippi Academy of Sciences. He has written on ancient skepticism, the nature of time, the history of biology, the concept of sovereignty, how science and law influence one another, and has contributed to *Mr. Monk and Philosophy: The Curious Case of the Defective Detective* (2010). Like Plankton, he often finds himself concocting nefarious schemes, and if his ego is ever bruised he tends to scream at those around him, reminding them that "I went to college!!!"

TIMOTHY DUNN is an assistant professor of philosophy at the University of Wisconsin—Waukesha. He has contributed chapters to *The Philosophy of the X-Files* (2009) and *Steven Spielberg and Philosophy* (2008) as well as the award-winning *Homer Simpson Goes to Washington: American Politics through Popular Culture* (2008). His current research interests include egoism and consumer ethics. After becoming a fan of *SpongeBob SquarePants*, he realized that most of what he learned in college about marine biology is hopelessly out of date.

DENISE DU VERNAY is the co-author of *The Simpsons in the Classroom: Embiggening the Learning Experience with the*

Wisdom of Springfield (2010). She has been teaching courses in literature, composition, speech, and humanities since 1999. Denise is particularly interested in popular culture and social media, and has written about pedagogy for *USA Today online*, social media and television for Splitsider.com, and linguistics for the Macmillan dictionary. When she's not writing or watching television, Denise is in the kitchen perfecting her Krabby Patty recipe.

JOSEPH J. FOY is an assistant professor at the University of Wisconsin-Parkside. Foy is the editor of the John G. Cawelti Award-winning book *Homer Simpson Goes to Washington: American Politics through Popular Culture* (2009) and co-editor of the follow-up *Homer Simpson Marches on Washington: Dissent through American Popular Culture* (2010). Foy has also contributed essays to *The Philosophy of the X-Files* (2009), *Steven Spielberg and Philosophy* (2008), *True Blood and Philosophy* (2010), and *The Philosophy of Joss Whedon* (2011). In his spare time, Foy sits with Jack Kahuna Laguna staring all night into the fire hoping that all secrets will be revealed.

WILSON GONZÁLEZ-ESPADA is an Associate Professor of Science at Morehead State University in Kentucky. He has taught courses in general education physical science, physics, inquiry physical science for teachers, and science methods. His research interests include physics education, science assessment, the nature of science, and the public understanding of science. Dr. González-Espada is a frequent science fair judge and an active member of Ciencia Puerto Rico, where he promotes scientific literacy on the Island. He regularly contributes papers or posters at professional meetings, and has published both scholarly and newspaper articles, but never in the *Krabby Kronicle*.

ROBERT JACOB KINCAID is currently attending Morehead State University and will soon graduate with degrees in English and Philosophy. Afterward he plans to work on his Master's in the Art of Teaching and then teach high-school English. He delivered pizzas in high school, but often got lost because he didn't know any of the old pioneer tricks.

NATASHA LIEBIG is a professor at the University of South Florida. She works in nineteenth- and twentieth-century Continental philosophy with special research in phenomenology, embodiment, and aesthetics. She is currently presenting her work on trauma, embodiment, and metaphor at various conferences around the world. She likes to lovingly remind her students that no matter how much they try, they can't fool her—she listens to Public Radio!

NICK MICHAUD went to college! He currently teaches philosophy at the University of North Florida and Florida State College Jacksonville. Nick's interests include world domination, enslavement of the masses, and crochet. You can find him regularly dining at the Chum Bucket helping Plankton plan to take over the world. What Plankton doesn't know is that Nick has no intention of sharing the power. . . .

NICOLE R. PRAMIK is an Adjunct English Instructor at Ashland Community and Technical College. She dabbles in science fiction and fantasy and makes use of popular culture in the classroom. After a long, hard day of grading papers and writing fiction, she enjoys downing a Triple Goober Berry Sunrise sundae or two.

ROBERT VUCKOVICH has a BA in philosophy from Wilfrid Laurier University and is in talks with one university program in the hope of earning a Master's degree in philosophy by working on a thesis on Diogenes of Sinope and sexual ethics. He has written "The Art of Rhetorical Deception and Modification" for the collection, *Rhetoric, Uncertainty and the University as Text: How First Year Students Construct the Academic Experience*, and "*Evangelion* and Existentialism: the Case of Shinji Ikari" for the collection, *Everyday Fantastic: Essays on Science Fiction and Human Being*. When he is not philosophizing on animated issues, he is trying to land employment at the Chum Bucket, so that he can earn enough money to go back to the Philippines and locate Bikini Bottom, which is somewhere around Manila Bay.

SHAUN P. YOUNG is Senior Policy Associate at the Mowat Centre for Policy Innovation at the University of Toronto. He's also a sessional lecturer at the University of Ontario Institute of Technology. Shaun's research interests focus on issues of justice in multicultural societies. He is the author or editor of four books and fourteen journal articles in the fields of political philosophy and public policy. Shaun neither requires nor requests that his students call him "Mr. Doctor Professor Shaun."

NATHAN ZOOK is an associate professor of political science at Montgomery College where he co-ordinates the International Studies program. His work has appeared in *Homer Simpson Goes to Washington: American Politics through Popular Culture* (2009) and numerous encyclopedias. He lives in Washington, DC, and frequents restaurants in the Foggy Bottom neighborhood which happens to be a lot less classy than Bikini Bottom—it lacks a good Krusty Krab franchise.

Index